Legendary
Artists and Entertainers

Their Lives and Gravesites

VOLUME 2

JOE FARRELL AND **JOE FARLEY**
WITH LAWRENCE KNORR

SUNBURY PRESS
Mechanicsburg, PA USA

Published by Sunbury Press, Inc.
Mechanicsburg, Pennsylvania

SUNBURY
PRESS
www.sunburypress.com

For information about special discounts for bulk purchases, please contact Sunbury Press Orders Dept. at (855) 338-8359 or orders@sunburypress.com.

To request one of our authors for speaking engagements or book signings, please contact Sunbury Press Publicity Dept. at publicity@sunburypress.com.

FIRST SUNBURY PRESS EDITION: February 2023

Set in Adobe Garamond Pro | Interior design by Crystal Devine | Cover by Lawrence Knorr | Edited by Lawrence Knorr.

Publisher's Cataloging-in-Publication Data
Names: Farrell, Joe, author | Farley, Joe, author | Knorr, Lawrence, author.
Title: Legendary artists and entertainers : their lives and gravesites volume 2 / Joe Farrell and Joe Farley with Lawrence Knorr.
Description: First trade paperback edition. | Mechanicsburg, PA : Sunbury Press, 2023. | Includes biographical references and index.
Summary: Joe Farrell, Joe Farley, and Lawrence Knorr have combed New York and Pennsylvania for more gravesites and biographies of some of our most interesting and accomplished authors, musicians, actors, and entertainers.
Identifiers: ISBN 979-8-88819-057-9 (softcover) | ISBN 979-8-88819-058-6 (ePub).
Subjects: BIOGRAPHY & AUTOBIOGRAPHY / Music | BIOGRAPHY & AUTOBIOGRAPHY / Entertainment & Performing Arts | BIOGRAPHY & AUTOBIOGRAPHY / Rich & Famous.

Product of the United States of America
0 1 1 2 3 5 8 13 21 34 55

Continue the Enlightenment!

Contents

Introduction

In the introduction to *Volume One* of *Legendary Artists and Entertainers*, I wrote that we hoped the response would encourage us to do *Volume Two*. Well, it did, and here it is. I, for one, think it is better than *Volume One*. It contains many stories worthy of your attention, from the celebrated life of superstar Lucille Ball to the incredible story of the under-celebrated courageous Nellie Bly.

Twenty-six new chapters tell the tragic life of influential jazz singer Billie Holiday and the tragic premature death of inspirational singer, songwriter, and social activist Harry Chapin. Also, read about the unusual lives of two unusual men of comedy, Andy Kaufman and Soupy Sales. There are chapters on Broadway legends George M. Cohan, critically acclaimed Pittsburgh playwright August Wilson, and iconic dancer, singer and actor Bill "Bojangles" Robinson.

We had plenty to write about, and looking at the Contents page will whet your appetite. There is no sense in listing anymore of them here.

Oh yeah—there's Fred Rogers and John Lennon too!

Joe Farrell
February 2023

1

Nick Adams

"Johnny Yuma Was a Rebel"

County: Columbia • Town: Berwick
Buried at Saints Cyril and Methodius Ukrainian Cemetery
706 North Warren Street

He was an actor who appeared in several significant films, including *Mister Roberts, Giant,* and *Rebel Without a Cause.* He was nominated for an Academy Award for Best Supporting Actor in the 1963 film *Twilight of Honor,* but the award went to Melvyn Douglas. He is best known for playing the role of Johnny Yuma in the television series *The Rebel.* His name was Nick Adams.

Adams was born Nicholas Aloysius Adamshock on July 10, 1931, in Nanticoke, Pennsylvania. His father, Peter Adamshock, was a Ukrainian-born coal miner. When Adams was five years old, his uncle was killed in a mining accident, and as a result, Adams's father moved the family to Jersey City, New Jersey.

Peter Adamshock got a job as a janitor in an apartment building. One of the perks of the job was that it came with living quarters in the basement. During this period, Adams's mother went to work for Western Electric.

When young Nick was still in high school, he received an offer from the Saint Louis Cardinals to play minor league baseball. He turned that offer down because he didn't feel the job paid enough. It's been said that as a teenager, he made money by hustling pool games. Money was important to him. When his father urged him to pursue a trade, he responded by saying he wanted to do something where he could make a lot of money and that he couldn't do that with a trade. So, it could be said that the pursuit of wealth is what led to his decision to get into acting.

Photo of Nick Adams in a guest-starring role on the television program
The Monroes.

In 1947 Adams, who was 17 at the time, visited New York City. He went into a theater where an audition was being held for a play called *The Silver Tassie*. It was here that he met the actor Jack Palance who, like Adams, hailed from the coal country of northeastern Pennsylvania and was of Ukrainian descent. When Palance asked Adams why he wanted to be an actor, the answer he got was for the money. Palance, who had changed his name from Jack Palahniuk, introduced Adams to the director as Nick Adams. Adams failed to land a part in the play, but Palance directed him to a junior theater group where he got an acting job playing the role of Muff Potter in *Tom Sawyer*. During this time, Adams auditioned for a role in the play Mister Roberts where he met the legendary actor Henry Fonda. Fonda advised Adams to take some acting lessons. After a year in New York City, Adams hitchhiked across the country to Los Angeles.

Once he reached Los Angeles, Adams worked as a doorman, usher, and maintenance man at the Warners Theater in Beverly Hills. His first paid acting job was in a stage play called *Mr. Big Shot*. His first film role came in 1951 in a movie titled *Somebody Loves Me*. The following year he was drafted into the United States Coast Guard.

In June of 1954, Adams auditioned in his Coast Guard uniform for the famed director John Ford. The effort earned him the part of Seaman Reber in the film *Mister Roberts*. Adams completed his military service, and upon his return to Los Angeles, based on his work in *Mister Roberts*, he signed a contract with the Warner Brothers studio.

In 1955 Adams landed a role in the movie *Rebel Without a Cause*. He befriended the stars of the movie James Dean and Natalie Wood. During breaks in the filming, Dean and Adams would entertain the cast by imitating movie stars such as Marlon Brando. When Dean was killed in an automobile accident in 1955, Adams overdubbed some of Dean's lines for the film *Giant*. Adams attempted to cash in on Dean's death by writing articles about Dean for movie magazines. Also, he claimed that he had adopted Dean's habits when it came to fast cars, claiming he had been arrested for speeding nine times in one year.

In the late 1950s, Adams's career began to blossom. He appeared in several successful television shows such as *Wanted: Dead or Alive*, which starred Steve McQueen. Also, he appeared in films, including *No Time for Sergeants* and *Pillow Talk*.

In 1959 Adams was cast to star in a television series titled *The Rebel*. Adams's character was named Johnny Yuma, an ex-Confederate soldier who wandered through the west toting a sawed-off shotgun. Adams had hoped to get his friend Elvis Presley to sing the title song for the show, but the producer picked Johnny Cash. The show was a hit, and 76 half-hour episodes were filmed before it was canceled at the end of the 1961 season.

In 1964 Adams appeared in an episode of the television show *The Outer Limits*. Critics would later point to this performance as proof that he was underrated as an actor. In 1964 he co-starred in the movie *Young Dillinger,* but the critics panned the movie, and it flopped.

It was around this time that Adams's career began to go downhill. In 1965, after publicly declaring that he would not work on films that were produced outside the United States, he accepted parts in Japanese science fiction films including *Frankenstein Conquers the World* and the 6th Godzilla film *Invasion of Astro-Monster*. During this period, he also starred in a film with Boris Karloff that was filmed in England called *Die, Monster, Die!* In 1967 Adams would appear in a Disney release titled *Mosby's Marauders*. He also appeared in some television series, including *The Wild Wild West* and *Combat*. In 1968 he was cast to star in a low budget science fiction film called *Mission Mars,* which critics described as being "utterly dreadful." His last production in the United States was a stock car movie titled *Fever Heat*. His last appearance on film was in a Spanish language western called *Los Asesinos*.

Adams married a former child actress named Carol Nugent in 1959. The couple had two children, Allyson Lee Adams and Jeb Stuart Adams. The relationship between Adams and his wife was a rocky one. By 1965, they were separated, and the children were living with Carol. In November of 1966, Carol initiated divorce proceedings and obtained a restraining order against Adams.

On the night of February 7, 1968, Adams failed to show up for a dinner appointment he had made with his lawyer, Erwin Roeder. Roeder drove to Adams's Beverly Hills home to check on the actor. He broke a window to gain entry and found Adams in his upstairs bedroom in a sitting position leaning against a wall dead. Adams was 36 years old.

The coroner, Dr. Thomas Noguchi, determined that the cause of death was "paraldehyde and promazine intoxication." He was unable to determine if the death was accidental or a suicide. Over the years, Adams's

*Unique grave of the underrated movie and TV star
Nick Adams.*

children have speculated that foul play may have been involved in the death of their father. Adams's best friend, actor Robert Conrad, has always felt that the death was accidental. Adams was laid to rest in the Saints Cyril and Methodius Ukrainian Cemetery in Berwick, Pennsylvania.

Adams's death at such a young age has made him part of what's been called the curse of *Rebel Without a Cause*. The curse is based on the fact that four of the cast members of that film passed away at a very young age. As mentioned previously, in addition to Adams, James Dean died in an automobile accident at the age of 24. Another star in the movie was Sal Mineo, who was stabbed to death on February 12, 1976, while he was walking home from a rehearsal for a play. He was 37 years old. Finally, the female lead in the movie, Natalie Wood, drowned on February 28, 1981. Wood was 43 years old at the time of her death.

If You Go:

The authors suggest a visit to the O'Donnell Winery located at 25 Hayes Road in Berwick. The wines are tasty, and the owners are very friendly and eager to do all they can to meet your needs. Besides, weather permitting, there is outside seating in a beautiful setting where you can watch the Susquehanna River flow by as you enjoy the fine wines.

The authors with Norbert O'Donnell, the owner of the O'Donnell winery in Berwick.

2

Lucille Ball

"We All Love Lucy"

County: Chautauqua • Town: Jamestown, New York
Buried at Lake View Cemetery
907 Lakeview Avenue

Numerous awards and honors were showered on the subject of this chapter. She has two stars on the Hollywood Walk of Fame. She was nominated for thirteen Primetime Emmy Awards and emerged as the winner five times. She was presented with the Golden Globe Cecil B. DeMille Award and the Women in Film Crystal Award. She received the Lifetime Achievement Award from the Kennedy Center Honors. The Academy Of Television Arts And Sciences honored her with the Governor's Award. She was also inducted into the Television Hall of Fame. She labored as a model, actress, singer, comedian, and producer. Her name was Lucille Ball, but to her countless fans, she was simply Lucy.

Lucy was born on August 6, 1911, in Jamestown, New York. Her father, Henry Durrell, worked as a lineman for Bell Telephone. Her mother, Desiree, known as DeDe, was a pianist. As a result of her father's profession, the family frequently moved when Lucy was a young child. One of Lucy's biographers, Kathleen Brady, in *Lucille The Life of Lucille Ball* describes the youngster as "lively, talkative and fearless." During her first years, Lucy lived in Montana and then in a neighborhood outside Detroit, Michigan, where her father worked for the Michigan Bell Company.

When Lucy was six months shy of her fourth birthday, her mother was pregnant with her second child. Lucy's father came down with typhoid fever. The disease proved fatal, and his daughter had little memory

Lucille Ball

of her dad. Lucy's mother returned to New York, where her maternal grandparents assisted in raising her and her brother.

Four years after Lucy's father's death, her mother married Edward Peterson. Lucy was left under the care of Peterson's parents while the newlyweds went to Detroit, where Peterson had a job that was supposed to last six months. The couple returned in 1922. Lucy, her mother, and stepfather moved back in with Lucy's grandparents, who had purchased a home in Celoron, New York, a resort village located on Chautauqua Lake. Lucy was twelve then and loved her new home at 59 West 8th Street (it would later be renamed Lucy Lane). The house on 8th Street reunited the family. Lucy joined her brother Fred (who had remained under the care of his stepfather's parents), her aunt Lola, and her three-year-old cousin, Cleo. Lucy loved Celoron, where one could find a boardwalk with a ramp to the lake that the children would use as a slide. There was also a roller coaster, a bandstand, and a stage where vaudeville performers appeared.

Fred would later recall life in Celoron. "We all worked all the time. And we had chickens and pigeons and pigs, and Lucy kept track of the house and all of the cleaning and some of the cooking. Bossy she was. In charge she was." However, when Lucy wasn't working or at school, she would get Fred and Cleo together and lead them in little plays and comedies for anyone who would watch.

The young girl became very interested in acting. Encouraged by her stepfather, she tried out and won a part chorus for summer performances at the Chautauqua Institution. Her biographer describes Lucy as "craving for attention." She found that performing was a way to gain attention and praise. She began to dream about performing on bigger stages than the ones available near Jamestown. Against her mother's wishes, she began making multiple trips to Manhattan, hoping to land a job in vaudeville or on Broadway. At fifteen, she traveled to New York and enrolled in the Robert Milton-John Anderson School of Drama. Her stay in the school was a short one. Her instructors were not impressed with her talents. Looking back on the experience, Lucy said, "All I learned in drama school was how to be frightened."

Lucy wasn't alone in not making it at the school. At the time, the star student was Bette Davis, who Lucy found intimidating. Based on Davis's memoirs, new students were reminded daily that they had chosen the toughest, least glamorous life possible and offered only sweat, jealousy, competition, disillusionment, and insecurity. "We were constantly at work, rehearing and memorizing while we forged ahead with our studies." Davis started in a class of seventy and finished in a class of twelve.

Lucy's failure at the school didn't crush her ambition. She continued to try out for parts on Broadway and with the Ziegfeld Follies. Her big break came when she landed a modeling job as a Chesterfield Girl for the cigarette company. Her picture appeared in magazines and on a Times Square billboard. These photos caught the attention of a talent agent, Sylvia Hahlo, who sent her to Hollywood to appear in a 1933 musical starring Eddie Cantor titled *Roman Scandals.*

Lucy had arrived in Hollywood with a six-week contract. When she arrived at the movie set, she saw that she was just one of many beautiful models. In an effort to stand out, she took crepe paper and placed pieces on her face. When Cantor saw her, he burst out laughing. After he got it under control, he said, "That Ball dame—she's a riot."

Although she only had a small part in the movie and had to fight to get one speaking line, the movie mogul Samuel Goldwyn extended her contract. Despite the contract extension, Lucy was still only getting small parts. Still, her efforts were noticed. One executive at the studio recalled, "She was one of dozens of girls at the studio and waiting for an opportunity. The difference was that she was a worker. That, and Jesus, what energy!"

Like many young actresses, Lucy had to deal with the casting couch. As detailed in her biography, one day on the set, a note was delivered to her from what she described as an "old guy who wants me to come up to his office." She said to the actor George Murphy, "What do you suppose he wants me to come up to his office for?"

Murphy said, "Lucille, I'd rather not think about it."

She responded, "Don't, because I'm not going."

Wanting credited parts, she signed with Columbia Pictures, where she appeared in a 1934 Three Stooges vehicle *Three Little Pigskins.* Reflecting on the part, she said, "I didn't know what I was getting into." It was classic Stooges slapstick with Moe, Larry, and Curly hitting her with pies and spraying her with seltzer. Lucy was often asked what she learned from working with the Stooges. She said they taught her that seltzer is painful if squirted up one's nose. The part did earn her the first film credit of her career.

Lucy was pleased with her progress at Columbia and was surprised when she was let go when the studio cut back on its contracts. She heard from a friend that RKO was doing a movie set in a Paris fashion house and was looking for girls with modeling experience. She auditioned and was one of five models hired to appear in *Roberta,* starring Irene Dunne and a brand new dance team made up of Fred Astaire and Ginger Rogers.

In 1937 Lucy got a big break when she was cast to appear in the movie *Stage Door.* She played Judy Canfield, a wisecracking member of a group of aspiring actresses. Other cast members included Katherine Hepburn, Ginger Rogers, Ann Miller, and Adolphe Menjou. Lucy held Hepburn in awe. She recalled, "The very way she talked was terrifying to me. She didn't talk to me directly, so it didn't matter, but I was riveted to her. So was everyone else. She was beautiful and not standoffish. She just ignored the whole set."

Actually, Hepburn did take notice of Lucy. Reminiscing about her, she observed, "I don't think Lucille in any way thought she was beautiful, and at the beginning of her career, no one else did. She had 'it.' She was always an amusing creature, and she was funny on her own. She had a lot of spunk."

The following year Lucy appeared with the Marx Brothers in the film *Room Service.* By this time, the brothers' best work was behind them. The critic John Mosher wrote, "As comic pictures go, this ranks certainly above average; it has enough of the Marxian note for that. As Marx Brothers movies go, however, it is a minor effort."

Lucy did impress the film's director, who observed, "Like most good actresses, she didn't like to be directed. She didn't need to be. She was her own self. It has to be carefully remembered these are stars, and there are actresses. Movies are just interested in great personalities. I think Lucy was a great, great personality."

During this period, Lucy was also doing radio work. Reflecting on her efforts in this media, she maintained that it helped sharpen her skills. "This gave me a name in the trade as a good feminine foil. I could flip a comedy line, which a lot of actresses couldn't do. In radio, I couldn't rely on props or costumes or makeup; I had to rely on timing and tone of voice for comic effects, and this was invaluable training."

Lucy decided to visit New York, where some friends recommended that she take in the Broadway show *Too Many Girls.* The music for the play was composed by the very popular duo of Richard Rogers and Lorenz Hart. While she wasn't impressed with the show, there was an actor who caught her eye. She recalled that when he began singing "Tempt Me Not," "I couldn't take my eyes off this Desi Arnaz. Striped football jersey hugged his big shoulders and chest, while those narrow hips in tight football pants swayed to the catchy rhymes of the bongo drum he was carrying. I recognized the kind of electrifying charm that can never be faked star quality."

In 1940 Desi arrived in Hollywood to repeat his Broadway role as a football star in the movie version of *Too Many Girls.* Lucy had also been cast in the film as Connie, a wealthy coed. George Abbott had been chosen to direct the film, and when Lucy saw him in the studio commissary, she went over to say hello. Abbott introduced Lucy to Desi, who was also present. Lucy, at the time, was filming *Dance, Girl, Dance,* where she played the part of a tough burlesque dancer. She was dressed in a showy gold dress and sported a black eye that had been applied to her for a fight scene. Desi wasn't impressed; he said she "looked like a two-dollar whore who had been badly beaten up by her pimp." His view changed when he saw Lucy cleaned up, remarking to a fellow actor, "Man, that is a hunk of woman. She sure doesn't look anything like she did this morning."

Whether it was love at first sight, as some believe, there is no doubt that the romantic nature of their relationship blossomed during the filming of *Too Many Girls.* The actor Van Johnson observed, "She fell in love with him and his accent and his dark, dark beauty." There was one complication; Desi was engaged at the time. During the filming, he took his fiancée to a party thrown by Eddie Bracken for members of the cast at his Malibu beach house. When Lucy saw Desi, she patted the sand beside her and told him to sit down, which he did. By the end of the evening, Desi's engagement was a thing of the past. *Too Many Girls* was released on October 8, 1940. Less than two months later, on November 30, 1940, Lucy and Desi celebrated their marriage.

On December 7, 1941, the Japanese attack on Pearl Harbor brought the United States into World War II. At the beginning of the war, Desi joined a Victory Caravan with other stars, including Bob Hope and Mickey Rooney. Then he was drafted into the army, where he served until 1945. During this time, Lucy also entertained the troops and sold war bonds while continuing to appear in films.

In 1942 she appeared in what she would later call her favorite film, *The Big Street.* She played the part of a self-centered nightclub performer who is paralyzed after her gangster boyfriend acting in a fit of rage, pushes her down a flight of stairs. Lucy sought advice before accepting the role because she was worried that audiences would believe she was actually like the character in the movie. She talked to the actor Charles Laughton who agreed that the part created a challenge. He urged her to take the part, saying, "If you are going to play a bitch, play the bitchiest bitch who ever lived, or don't play the part at all." Her performance impressed many critics. James Agee wrote in *Time* magazine that she "tackles her emotional role as if it were a sirloin and she didn't care who was looking." *Life* magazine said, "Ball's performance is superb—the girl can really act." Unfortunately, the film was a box office dud and served as a sign that her days at RKO were soon to end.

Lucy made one more film for RKO before signing with Metro-Goldwyn-Mayer (MGM). Sydney Guillaroff, the legendary hairstylist for the studio, decided that Lucy needed a change. He found her brown hair uninteresting and unsuitable for the new Technicolor films. He remarked, "The hair is brown, but the soul is on fire," and dyed her locks tango red.

Her first film at MGM was *Du Barry Was a Lady* with Red Skelton and Gene Kelly. It was a musical comedy, and though Lucy insisted, "I can't sing! I can't dance!" she responded well when the choreographer told her, "You can, just stop wasting time saying you can't and get it done." The film was a box office success.

Meanwhile, Desi, who had a reputation as a serial womanizer, was up to his old tricks and putting a strain on the marriage. Lucy was convinced he was fooling around and decided to get a divorce. The Associated Press covered the story under the title "Red-Head Asks Divorce." On the day she got her interlocutors decree, she reconciled with Desi, negating the process. Recalling the period, she said, "I closed my eyes, put blinders on, and ignored what was too painful to think about."

By the late forties, Lucy had been working in the motion picture business for 15 years. She had appeared in more than 60 films but remained unhappy with her career status. She was never able to land many of the roles she wanted. Looking to make a change, she decided to go back into radio. It would prove to be a wise decision.

On July 5, 1948, CBS radio broadcast what was to be a one-time special titled *My Favorite Husband* starring Lucy and Lee Bowman. The response to the program prompted the network to turn the show into a series. Bowman wasn't available, and he was replaced by Richard Denning, who played the part of Lucy's husband. The show was a hit, and there was little doubt that Lucy was in charge. The writing partners Madelyn Pugh and Bob Carroll Jr. were brought in to write the scripts. The duo found Lucy to be extremely demanding. Pugh recalled, "I think someone told her to come on strong and to run the show. She was trying to do that, and it was terrifying at first." CBS then hired Jess Oppenheimer to control Lucy and run things. A total of 124 episodes of the show aired from July 23, 1948, through March 31, 1951.

Meanwhile, Buster Keaton, who had always been a fan of Lucy and called her the best comedienne in Hollywood, succeeded in getting Columbia to sign her to a contract in 1949. Her first film for Columbia was *Miss Grant Takes Richmond,* followed by *The Fuller Brush Girl* featuring Eddie Albert as a co-star. Lucy obviously impressed Albert, who said, "Lucille was more devoted to her career and talent than anyone else I ever met. She thought only of being an entertainer. The ego of it was amazing! She sought out opportunities to do stunts and kept asking, 'Can I do it?' She'd roll barrels and bowling balls and got blown up in the stunts. She was in smoke and fire. She was so stalwart. I was glad it was her and not me."

The film itself proved to be a success that showcased her talents. *Variety* observed, "If there were ever any doubts as to Miss Ball's forte, *Fuller Brush Girl* dispels them. She is an excellent comedienne, and in this rowdy incoherent yarn, with its Keystone Kop overtones, she garners major laurels."

According to her biographer, Lucy's performance in *The Fuller Brush Girl* brought her to the attention of the renowned director Cecil B. de Mille. He decided to cast her in *The Greatest Show on Earth*. The part he had in mind was Angel, the elephant girl who rides the animal and allows herself to be curled up in the elephant's trunk. Lucy wanted the part badly, but the Columbia movie mogul Harry Cohn didn't want to release her from her contract, hoping to save money by forcing her to break it. However, she found out she was pregnant, which made her appearance in the film impossible. According to Desi, who accompanied her to see de Mille to give him the news, the director turned to him and said, "Congratulations, Mr. Arnaz. You are the only man who has ever screwed his wife, Cecil B. de Mille, Paramount Pictures, and Harry Cohn, all at the same time."

Despite her success at Columbia, Lucy never achieved the top rank of stardom in motion pictures. Indeed, her most notable success was her radio show. However, by the early 1950s, many radio personalities like Milton Berle and George Burns were moving to television. She also believed that she could work with Desi in the new medium, which would keep him at home. According to Lucy, what finally convinced her to give it a go was a dream in which the late actress Carole Lombard appeared before her and said, "Honey, go ahead. Give it a whirl."

By this time, Lucy and Desi had already formed their own production company, which they named Desilu productions. The duo hoped to create a television series and sell it to CBS. The original idea was to take *My Favorite Husband* to the small screen with Lucy and Desi playing the leads. CBS executives didn't like the idea. They thought that the idea of Desi playing a midwestern banker was ridiculous.

To prove CBS wrong, the couple developed a vaudeville act which they performed at New York's historic Ritz Theater with Desi's orchestra.

It was a hit, and CBS executive Harry Ackerman decided that the Ball-Arnaz pairing was worth a shot. A pilot was ordered, and Lucy and Desi used her radio writing team of Oppenheimer, Pugh, and Carroll to create the series that was named *I Love Lucy*. The show was set in a New York apartment building where Lucy Ricardo (Ball) and her singer-bandleader husband Ricky Ricardo resided with their best friends and landlords Fred Mertz (William Frawley) and Ethel Mertz (Vivian Vance). The show was designed to allow Lucy to display her talents at clowning and physical comedy.

I Love Lucy made its debut on October 15, 1951. The show's sponsor was Philip Morris. The company's president, O. Parker McComas, tuned in but wasn't entertained calling it "unfunny." He's told his ad people to cancel the deal, but they convinced him to wait a week. As it turned out, McComas may have been a minority of one. Americans loved the show. NBC executive Mike Dann tuned in to check out the competition. His network aired almost all of television's top shows. He recalled, "I watched the show that night to be sure we would retain our leadership. By 9:30 on a Monday night, I knew my job was in jeopardy." *I Love Lucy* was a hit.

The series ran until May 6, 1957. Those six seasons produced 180 half-hour episodes. In four of the six seasons, it was the most-watched show in the United States. It was the first show to end while sitting on the top of the Nielsen ratings. It has been syndicated in dozens of languages around the globe and remains popular in America. In 2013, CBS showed a colorized version of a Christmas episode that drew an audience of more than eight million, 62 years after the show premiered. The show won five Emmy Awards and is regarded as one of the most influential sitcoms in history. In 2012, it was voted the Best TV Show of All Time in a survey conducted by ABC News and *People* magazine.

A modified version of the show ran from 1957 to 1960 titled *The Lucille Ball-Desi Arnaz Show*. The format here called for one-hour specials, and 13 were made. They were later shown as reruns under the title *The Lucy-Desi Comedy Hour*.

During the years they worked together on television, the couple had two children, Lucie Arnaz and Desi Arnaz Jr. While things were going great for the Ricardos, the same could not be said for Lucy and Desi's marriage. Their daughter Lucy recalled, "I think they would have loved to have been the Ricardos, who had ways of kissing and making up. I think they both found it extraordinarily hard to say, 'I'm sorry.'"

By the end of the 1950s, Lucy had grown weary of Desi's drinking, gambling, and womanizing. After the success of *I Love Lucy* and its sequel, the duo decided to bring the series to an end in 1960. *Life Magazine* described the making of the final show in the Lucille Ball tribute issue:

During the filming, Desi and Lucy weren't speaking to one another. "Everyone just wanted to get through it, get it done, get it in the can," said Edie Adams, who appeared on the show with Ernie Kovacs. In the final scene, Ricky kisses Lucy. "It was a kiss that would wrap up 20 years of love and friendship, triumphs and failures, ecstasy and sex, jealousy and regrets, heartbreaks and laughter . . . and tears," Desi wrote in his autobiography, *A Book*. "The only thing we were not able to hide were the tears." After they had delivered their final lines, Lucy and Desi stood and looked at each other in silence. "You're supposed to say 'cut,'" Lucy told her husband of nearly 20 years with tears in her eyes. "I know, "Desi responded. "Cut, goddam it!" He left for Las Vegas, and the following day she drove to the Santa Monica Superior Court And filed for divorce.

Although her marriage had ended, her career as an actress and businesswoman continued. In business, Lucy bought out Desi's holdings in Desilu in 1962. She ran the company successfully for several years before selling it in 1968 for $17 million, the equivalent of approximately $140 million today. She also appeared on Broadway, in movies, and her own successful television series.

Shortly before her divorce, Lucy starred in the Broadway musical *Wildcat*. It would mark her only performances on a Broadway stage. The show sold well, but it was not a critical success. The reviews were lukewarm, and Lucy suffered from a virus and chronic fatigue during the show's 171-performance run. One bright spot came when her co-star Paula Stewart introduced her to the comic Gary Morton. Morton was 13 years younger than Lucy and told her he had never seen an episode of *I Love Lucy*. Still, the pair hit it off, and about a year and a half after her divorce became final, they were married at the Marble Collegiate Church in New York City.

Relative to her movie career in 1968, she starred with Henry Fonda in *Yours, Mine and Ours*. The duo had made one other film together in the 1940s; the difference this time was that it was Lucy who got top billing. She also starred in the 1974 musical *Mame*.

Despite these other ventures, the medium that provided her with the greatest success continued to be television. In October 1962, *The Lucy Show* made its debut. This was Lucy's third sitcom, which can be described as *I Love Lucy* without the husbands. Lucy played a widow, and Vivian Vance joined her again as a divorcée. Gale Gordon, who had worked with Lucy on radio, rounded out the cast. The show ran for six seasons and earned Lucy two Emmy Awards for Outstanding Lead Actress in a Comedy Series. Several celebrities made guest appearances, including Jack Benny, Dean Martin, George Burns, Joan Crawford, and Carol Burnett.

Burnett recalled that Lucy "knew the lights, the scenery, the costumes, the music, the makeup. Everything. And she was always right." Even though *The Lucy Show* ended the 1967-68 season ranked number two, Lucy decided to end the series as there were enough episodes for syndicated reruns.

After selling Desilu, Lucy started a new company called Lucille Ball Productions. She used that company to produce another television sitcom, *Here's Lucy*. In addition to Lucy, this series starred Gale Gordon and her two children, Desi Arnaz Jr. and Lucie Arnaz. This series ran from 1968 to 1974 and used numerous guest stars, including Ann Margaret, Johnny Carson, Vincent Price, Flip Wilson, Elizabeth Taylor, and Richard Burton. Burton didn't care for Lucy's rigid perfectionism and wasn't kind when he wrote about her in his memoir.

Lucy also starred in television specials, including *Lucy Calls the President* and *Lucy Moves to NBC*. She also appeared on the Carol Burnett

Lucille Ball grave - front

special *Carol + 2.* In addition to acting, in 1979, she became an assistant professor at California State University.

In 1986 she co-produced, with Gary Morton and Aaron Spelling, another sitcom *Life With Lucy,* which also starred her old friend Gale Gordon. This show failed and was canceled less than two months after its debut. In May of 1988, she entered the hospital after suffering a mild heart attack. Lucy made her last public appearance at the 1989 Academy Awards. She and her fellow presenter Bob Hope received a standing ovation.

Lucille Ball grave - back

In April 1989, Lucy was admitted to Cedars-Sinai Medical Center after experiencing chest pains. On April 26, she suffered an abdominal aortic aneurysm and passed away at 77. She was cremated, and her ashes were originally interned in the Forest Lawn Hollywood Hills Cemetery. In 2002 her remains were re-interred in the Hunt family plot at the Lake View Cemetery in Jamestown, New York.

3

John Barrymore

"The Great Profile"

County: Philadelphia • Town: Philadelphia
Buried at Mount Vernon Cemetery
3499 West Lehigh Avenue

He was born into an acting family. He first made a name for himself on stage, starting with light comedy and then appearing in dramas. He was especially praised for his work in Shakespearean plays. From the stage, he moved to the silver screen, where he met with immediate and great success. He was envied for his good looks, which earned him the moniker "the Great Profile." His name was John Barrymore.

Barrymore was born on February 15, 1882, in Philadelphia. His father, Herbert Arthur Chamberlayne Blythe, was a British actor who performed under the name Maurice Barrymore. His mother, Georgie Drew Barrymore, was an actress as well. Barrymore had a brother Lionel and a sister Ethel. His maternal grandmother was Louisa Lane Drew, who was also an actress and theatre manager. Drew was instrumental in directing all three siblings into acting. Growing up in such a theatrical family resulted in Barrymore meeting some of the leading actors of the day, including Edwin Booth.

While he was still in his teens, he dated the showgirl Evelyn Nesbitt (see the chapter on Harry Thaw in *Keystone Tombstones Volume Two*). There were rumors that Nesbitt had become pregnant and that Barrymore arranged for her to have an abortion. In 1906, Nesbitt's husband Harry Thaw shot one of her former lovers, the noted architect Stanford White, to death on the rooftop of Madison Square Garden. Questions were prepared to ask Barrymore at the trial, the purpose of which was to attack

John Barrymore

Nesbitt's character. The trial, however, was settled by an insanity plea, and Barrymore was never called to the stand.

Initially, Barrymore attempted to avoid following in his parent's footsteps by trying to make a living as a reporter and a cartoonist. He went to art school and worked for several New York newspapers before he decided to become an actor. He made his stage debut in 1903 at the Cleveland Theatre in Chicago. He then moved on to Broadway, where he performed for two years before heading to England to appear in a play called *The Dictator*.

John Barrymore

In 1906 Barrymore was staying in a hotel in San Francisco when the earthquake hit. He was starring in a production of *The Dictator* and was set to go to Australia to tour in that play. Barrymore had no desire to make that trip, so he went into hiding, spending the next few days at the house of a friend where he went on a drinking binge. While he was drinking, he came up with an idea as to how he could use the earthquake for his benefit. He posed as a reporter and made-up scenes he claimed to have witnessed. Years later, in a letter to his sister, he admitted he had done so. When the information became public, it did Barrymore no harm as, by that time, he was widely known and admired for his talent.

In 1910, Barrymore married an actress named Katherine Corri Harris. It was the first of his four marriages, and the couple divorced in 1917. By 1912, Barrymore was the actor who ruled the American stage. It was at this highpoint in his career that he decided to make motion pictures, transitioning away from working on Broadway. In 1913 he decided to abandon the stage to make films full time. That same year he starred in the silent film *An American Citizen*.

At first, Barrymore concentrated on making light comedies. A friend of his convinced him to try his hand at drama. In 1916 he appeared in a film called *Justice* to critical acclaim. One of his co-stars was Cathleen Nesbitt, who would introduce him to his second wife, Blanche Oelrichs. They would marry in 1920 and divorce in 1925. The union would produce one child, a daughter named Diana Blanche Barrymore. Diana would die at the age of 38 from an overdose of alcohol combined with sleeping pills. Barrymore later made a movie with Errol Flynn called *Too Much, Too Soon* based on her life.

When World War 1 saw the United States enter the fray in 1917, Barrymore, who was 35 at the time, tried to enlist in the armed forces. He failed the physical due to varicose veins. That same year he returned to Broadway to star in a play called *Peter Ibbetson* in a role his father had always wanted to play. In 1919 he starred with his brother Lionel in *The Jest*. Then it was back to Shakespeare when he appeared in *Richard III* in 1920. This was followed by what many consider his greatest stage triumph, his starring role in *Hamlet* in 1922. The play ran for 101 per-formances, and Barrymore broke the record for consecutive appearances that had been held by Edwin Booth.

Barrymore closed out his silent film career by appearing in several successful films. These included *Dr. Jekyll and Mr. Hyde* (the band Queen used scenes from this film in their music video "Under Pressure"), *Sherlock Holmes,* and *Don Juan.*

In 1928 he married the model and actress Dolores Costello. They were divorced in 1935. The union produced two children, a girl born in 1930 named Dolores Ethel Mae Barrymore and a son born in 1932 named John Drew Barrymore. John is the father of the actress Drew Barrymore.

Talking pictures proved to be a big plus for Barrymore. His debut in talkies was a dramatic reading of the Duke of Gloucester's speech from *Henry VI.* Barrymore's stage-trained voice fit perfectly with talk-ing pictures. In 1930 he reprised a role he had played in a silent film starring as Captain Ahab in *Moby Dick.* He then made a few movies with his brother Lionel including *Arsene Lupin, The Mad Genius,* and in 1932, *Grand Hotel.* The latter film featured an all-star cast that included Joan Crawford and Greta Garbo. That same year the brothers starred in *Rasputin and the Princess,* followed by *Dinner at Eight* in 1933.

Over the years, Barrymore appeared with most of the leading ladies of the time, including Myrna Loy, Katherine Hepburn, and Jean Harlow. In the 1933 film *Counsellor at Law,* Barrymore portrayed a Jewish attorney. The film critic Pauline Kael would later praise this performance calling it "one of the few screen roles that reveal his measure as an actor." She added that his "presence is apparent in every scene; so are his restraint, his humor, and his zest."

In the '30s, Barrymore's return to the stage met with much suc-cess. He inspired several plays, including *The Royal Family* and *My Dear Children.* Both plays would become films. He also served as the inspira-tion for two films, *Sing Baby Sing* and *The Great Profile.* In 1936 he gave a critically praised performance playing Mercutio in *Romeo and Juliet.* That same year he was married for the fourth and final time to Elaine Barrie, an actress. The two divorced in 1940.

In 1937 he appeared in a film with Jeanette MacDonald called *Maytime*. It became the top-grossing film of the year worldwide. It is still regarded as one of the best film musicals of the 1930s.

In the late '30s, Barrymore began losing the ability to remember his lines. As a result, when he made films, they were forced to use cue cards. His films began losing money, and by 1938 he was considered box office poison along with others such as Fred Astaire and Joan Crawford.

Barrymore collapsed while appearing on Rudy Vallee's radio show in 1942. He was rushed to the hospital. He had been a smoker his whole life and suffered from chronic alcoholism, heart problems, and pneumonia. According to one of his biographers, Barrymore roused and tried to say something to his brother Lionel, and Lionel asked him to repeat what he had said, and Barrymore replied, "You heard me, Mike." He then met death with a smile on May 29, 1942. According to Errol Flynn's memoirs, the film director Raoul Walsh took Barrymore's body and placed it in a chair in Flynn's house, left to be discovered by Flynn when he returned home from a night of drinking. Walsh said the story was true in a 1973 documentary called *The Men Who Made the Movies*. The story was challenged by a friend of Barrymore's who claimed that he and his son stayed with the body at the funeral right up to the burial. Among Barrymore's pallbearers were W. C. Fields, Louis B. Mayer, and David O. Selznick. He was laid to rest in Mount Vernon Cemetery in Philadelphia.

For his work in films, Barrymore was awarded a star on the Hollywood Walk of Fame. Unlike his sister Ethel and his brother Lionel, he never won an Academy Award. However, all three siblings have been inducted into the American Theatre Hall of Fame.

Barrymore was a good friend and drinking buddy of W. C. Fields. In the 1976 film, *W. C. Fields and Me*, Barrymore was portrayed by Jack Cassidy. He is also mentioned in the song "I May Be Wrong (But I Think You're Wonderful)" which was recorded by several artists including Doris Day.

If You Go:

What can we say except that attempting to visit this gravesite proved to be a first for us? I suppose we can begin by telling you that you need to call the cemetery at least 24 hours before your visit to make an appointment. This is necessary because the grounds are locked, and someone needs to meet you there for you to gain entrance. When we called, we spoke to a man who identified himself as the owner of the property. We informed him of who we wanted to visit, and he asked us if we were relatives. We told him no and explained the reason for our visit. He responded by telling us that we would need to pay a fee to photograph the grave. He said that, according to his attorney, the site was his intellectual property. We chose not to pay, so this marks the first grave included in this series that we were unable to visit. We hope our readers have better luck, and we continue to wonder what Drew Barrymore might think of the stand taken by the owner regarding our attempt to visit her grandfather's grave.

4

Nellie Bly

"Lonely Orphan Girl"

County: Bronx • Town: New York
Buried at Woodlawn Cemetery
517 East 233rd Street

Nellie Bly was an American journalist known for her investigative and undercover reporting. She was a pioneer in her field and launched a new kind of investigative journalism, earning acclaim in 1887 for her exposé of patients' treatment in an insane asylum and her trip around the world in 1889.

She was born Elizabeth Jane Cochran on May 5, 1864, in Cochran's Mills, Pennsylvania. Her father, Michael Cochran, founded the town. He was a judge and mill owner, whose first marriage produced ten children. After his first wife's death, Michael Cochran met and married a woman named Mary Jane, and together they had five kids of their own, the third of which was Elizabeth. Michael died suddenly when Elizabeth was six. His death was a terrible financial blow as he left no will to protect his second family's interests. Within a year of his death, Mary Jane had to auction off their home, and the family faced what can only be described as challenging times. She remarried three years later to a man who turned out to be abusive, and it ended in a tortuous divorce.

Elizabeth went to the Indiana Normal School (now Indiana University of Pennsylvania) in Indiana, Pennsylvania, at the age of 15, to train to become a teacher, one of the few professions open to women. She was forced to drop out because of a lack of funds for tuition. She then moved with her mother to Pittsburgh and helped run their house, which they opened to boarders.

Nellie Bly

In January 1885, Elizabeth read an article in the *Pittsburgh Dispatch* by Erasmus Wilson, Pittsburgh's most popular columnist. The article was entitled "What Girls Are Good For." Wilson wrote that women belonged in the home doing domestic tasks such as serving, cooking, and raising children. He called the working woman, "a monstrosity." The article admonished women for even attempting to gain an education or embark on a career. Elizabeth, familiar with the many young women who had to work to survive in industrial Pittsburgh, read the column with anger and wrote a fiery rebuttal which she signed "Lonely Orphan Girl." The paper's editor, George Madden, was so impressed with the anonymous writer's passion that he ran an ad asking her to identify herself.

When Elizabeth went to the newspaper's office and introduced herself, Madden offered her the chance to write a rebuttal piece for publication. She wrote an article called "The Girl Puzzle," and Madden was so impressed he offered her a full-time job. At the time, it was customary for female writers to use pennames. Madden gave Elizabeth hers: Nellie Bly, after a popular song by Stephen Foster, one of Pittsburgh's favorite songs. "Nellie" began her career as a reporter by writing about social issues, including labor laws and divorce law. She became known for her investigative and undercover reporting. She posed as a sweatshop worker to expose poor working conditions and wrote a series of articles about female factory workers. These exposés brought a lot of pressure on the paper from the business community to stop her.

She convinced the editors to allow her to visit Mexico and report on her experience. She spent nearly six months reporting on the lives and customs of the Mexican people. She uncovered political corruption, which she then revealed in her articles. In one, she protested a local journalist's imprisonment for criticizing the Mexican government (a dictatorship under Porfirio Diaz). She soon found herself threatened with arrest and left the country. Her accounts were later collected in the book *Six Months in Mexico.*

Despite her love of and success in investigative reporting, Bly's editors at the *Dispatch* relegated her to the paper's "women's pages." Frustrated with doing stories about fashion and flowers, she quit and moved to New York City in hopes of a more meaningful opportunity. She hoped to land a job at a major newspaper, but she was near broke after four months with no offers. She talked her way into the editor's office at Joseph Pulitzer's paper, the *New York World,* and got hired. The first assignment for the 23-year old was to feign insanity to investigate reports of brutality and neglect at the Women's Lunatic Asylum on Blackwell Island (now Roosevelt Island).

She began by checking into a boardinghouse and refusing to go to bed, claiming to be afraid of the other boarders. In the morning, the owners called the police, and when taken in front of a judge, Bly faked amnesia. (Ironically, a rival newspaper, the *New York Sun*, ran an article in its September 25, 1887, issue detailing her arrest, beneath the headline "Who Is This Insane Girl?") She was examined by several doctors who all declared her to be insane. The head of the Insane Unit at Bellevue Hospital pronounced her "undoubtedly insane," and she was committed to the asylum where she joined 1,600 other women. She experienced horrible food and undrinkable water, ice-cold baths, flimsy garments, and abusive treatment by the staff. Dangerous patients were tied together with rope. "What, excepting torture, would produce insanity quicker than this treatment?" she asked.

Photo of the great female investigative reporter.

After ten days, a *World* agent rescued her. On October 9, 1887, Nellie wrote the first of a two-part article detailing her experience, published in the Sunday edition of *The World* under the headline "Behind Asylum Bars." A week later, *The World* published part two, entitled "Inside the Mad House." The articles created a tremendous uproar. A grand jury launched an investigation into conditions at the asylum and invited Bly to assist. It turned out that many of the women were not mentally ill at all; some were immigrants who simply didn't know English and had trouble communicating. As a result, more money and needed reforms were instituted by the city. Her entire experience was published in book form in 1887 as *Ten Days in a Madhouse*.

Bly would spend the next several years writing articles for *The World*. She pioneered the field of investigative journalism. After going undercover, she exposed crooked lobbyists in government, tracked the plight of unwanted babies, reported on the conditions for factory workers, and arranged to be thrown into jail to expose female inmates' treatment. In 1894, she went to Chicago to cover the Pullman railroad strike and was the only reporter to tell the story from the strikers' perspective. Nellie Bly became so popular that *The World* would often use her name in the actual headline itself. People could not wait to see what she was up to next. Her fame also opened up doors of the rich and famous. She profiled boxer John L. Sullivan, suffragist Susan B. Anthony, and anarchist Emma Goldman.

NELLIE BLY'S BOOK

AROUND THE WORLD IN 72 DAYS

The famous reporter's own account of her astonishing, record-breaking, world-wide adventure.

EDITED BY IRA PECK

This is Bly's story of a trip that is still being writtten about to this day.

Her most famous exploit, however, was more like a stunt. In 1888, she proposed to her bosses at *The World* that she take a trip around the world, attempting to turn the fictional *Around the World in 80 Days* into fact for the first time. She wanted to beat Phileas Fogg's time, the hero of Jules Verne's massively popular 1873 novel. Her editor liked the idea, but the paper's business manager wanted to send a man.

"Very well," Bly said, "start the man, and I'll start the same day for some other newspaper and beat him."

The next year, a few months after her 25th birthday, the paper said "yes." She set sail on November 14, 1889, on the steamer *Augusta Victoria* heading east. Her journey took her to England, Egypt, Ceylon, Singapore, Hong Kong, and Japan. During a stop in France, she met Jules Verne, who encouraged her to beat the fictional record. *The World* promoted a hugely popular guessing contest to predict how many weeks/days/hours/minutes it would take her to complete the journey, offering a trip to Europe as first prize.

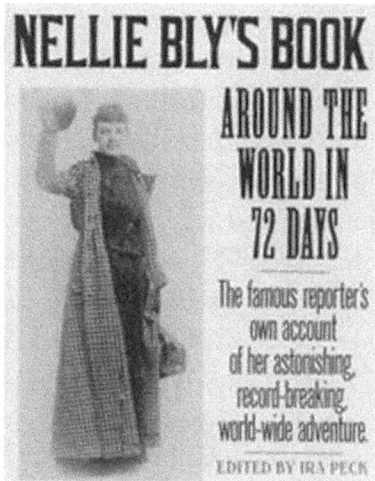

A new magazine called *Cosmopolitan* sent its reporter, Elizabeth Bisland, in the opposite direction to try to beat Bly around the globe, creating an actual race for all to follow. Bly sent short progress reports to the paper by cable and telegraph and more comprehensive reports by regular post, which ran weeks behind. Millions of people followed her journey, and it resulted in significantly increased newspaper readership. She traveled by ship, horse, rickshaw, sampan, burro, balloon, and more. When she reached Hong Kong, she learned that Bisland was ahead of her. Undaunted, Bly reached American soil in San Francisco on January 21, 1890, and boarded a private train chartered by Joseph Pulitzer. All along her journey eastward, she was met with cheering crowds.

Meanwhile, Bisland had missed her ship across the Atlantic and was still sailing westward from Europe on a different, slower ship when Bly's train pulled into New Jersey. When she stepped off the train at her official finish line in Jersey City, cannons boomed from the southern tip of Manhattan's Battery Park, and a large crowd roared. She had traveled around the world in 72 days, six hours, and 11 minutes. It would be four and a half more days before Bisland arrived.

Bly had earned international stardom for her months-long stunt. She turned her adventure into the 1890 book, *Nellie Bly's Book: Around the World in Seventy-Two Days.*

In 1895, Bly married millionaire manufacturer Robert Seaman. He was the owner of Iron Clad Manufacturing Company and 42 years her senior. As the marriage progressed, Nellie became more involved with the company and even patented a milk can of her design. When Seaman died in 1904, Nellie took over the company and became the world's leading female industrialist until employees' embezzlement led her into bankruptcy in 1914.

When World War I broke out, she returned to journalism and became America's first female war correspondent for the *New York Evening Journal.* She returned to New York in 1919 and regularly wrote for the *Evening Journal.*

Nellie Bly died of pneumonia at St. Mark's Hospital in New York City on January 27, 1922, at age 57. She continued to write her column

Gravesite of newspapers grand lady.

up until her death. She was buried in a modest grave in Woodlawn Cemetery in the Bronx. In 1978, the New York Press Club formally recognized Nellie and erected a monument at her grave.

If You Go:

Woodlawn Cemetery is itself a National Historic Landmark and contains over 300,000 interments. Its monuments, including over 1,300 mausoleums, were designed by legendary American architects, landscape designers, and sculptors. It contains the graves of many notables from all walks of life.

One such person is David Farragut (1801–1870), a Navy Admiral who received great acclaim for his service to the Union during the Civil War. He commanded the Union blockade of Southern ports, helped capture the Confederate city of New Orleans, and provided support for

General Grant's Vicksburg siege. He is best known for his victory at the Battle of Mobile Bay in August 1864. The bay was heavily mined (mines were called torpedoes in those days), and Farragut ordered his fleet to enter the bay. When one ship struck a mine, the others began to pull back, but Farragut rose to the occasion and famously proclaimed to "Damn the torpedoes, full speed ahead!" The fleet succeeded, and the heroic quote became famous. He was the first rear admiral, vice admiral, and admiral in the United States Navy.

Farragut died from a heart attack at 69 in Portsmouth, New Hampshire, on August 14, 1870. His grave is listed on the National Historic Register of Historic Places. Many destroyers have since been named USS *Farragut* in his honor, and he has been depicted on U.S. postage stamps three times.

Also buried in Woodlawn Cemetery is George Cohan (see Chapter 7).

5

Harry Chapin

"What Made America Famous"

County: Suffolk • Town: Huntington
Buried at Huntington Rural Cemetery
Address: 555 New York Avenue

Harry Chapin was a singer-songwriter and social activist who was, to his millions of fans, one of the most beloved performers in pop music history. His principal contribution was his "story song," a narrative form of song that owed much to older talking blues. These songs' subjects were often common people with tales of lost opportunities, cruel ironies, and life's hypocrisies. Clive Barnes of the *New York Post*, wrote "his songs were ballads to our time, memorials to his own generation. His words had a certain bitterness that reflected a nonacceptance of the world's imperfections." He did not write his story songs for the Top 40 charts, but because he had something to say.

He did more, however, than sing about his social concerns. He tried to do something about them. His involvement in humanitarian causes, the arts, and social organizations was extraordinary. Chapin was not just entertainment; he was an experience. "Not since Al Jolson," said Pete Seeger, "have I seen a performer who established such a natural rapport, empathy, and involvement with an audience." He performed more than 2,000 concerts throughout his career, and more than half of them were benefits. He raised more than six million dollars, which helped support more than 100 organizations, and he was only 38 when he died. "Harry was a rare occurrence," said Robert Redford. "There was nobody like him. I haven't met anybody with the degree of energy and the degree of commitment all tied into one force like him."

Harry Chaplin

Harry Forster Chapin was born on December 7, 1942, in Brooklyn, New York, to Jeanne Elspeth and Jim Chapin, a well-known percussionist. His parents divorced in 1950, with his mom getting custody of their four sons. Jim spent much of his time on the road playing with Tommy Dorsey and Woody Herman's bands. Harry's brothers, Tom and Steve, would also become musicians. His first formal introduction to music was singing in the Brooklyn Heights Boys Choir. Later, he learned to play the trumpet and then the guitar and banjo at the famed Greenwich House Music School. While singing in the choir, he met "Big" John Wallace, a tenor with a five-octave range, who later became his bassist, backing vocalist, and his straight man onstage.

When Harry was 15, he and his brothers formed their own folk band and played off and on at local clubs in Greenwich Village, calling themselves "The Chapin Brothers." He graduated from Brooklyn Tech in 1960 and enrolled at the United States Air Force Academy. He had chosen the Air Force Academy over Cornell and realized quickly, after arriving, that he had made a mistake. He transferred to Cornell to study architecture in the Fall of 1961. He dropped out of Cornell in 1964, without a degree, and was more interested in film than music. He began working in film-making, working his way up to editor, and eventually making the boxing documentary *The Legendary Champions* in 1968. The film won first prize at film festivals in New York and Atlanta and received an Academy Award nomination for Best Feature Documentary. He continued to work on music, and some of his songs were used in another documentary, *Blue Water, White Death*. In 1970, his brothers Steve and Tom reformed their band, and Harry provided them with songs.

Chapin met Sandy Gaston, a New York socialite, in 1966, when she called him asking for music lessons. They married two years later. Their meeting and romance is told in his song "I Wanna Learn a Love Song." Together they had two children, and he was stepfather to her three children from her previous marriage.

In 1971, Chapin was ready to go back to the music business in full force. His manager, Fred Kewley (who also managed his brothers), signed a five-week lease with the Village Gate in Greenwich Village to feature the Chapins (Tom and Steve). Harry decided he would like to be the opening act, and he and three band members rehearsed for a week in Kewley's office and arranged songs with cello parts and background vocals. They started opening for the Chapins. Several weeks later, he had attracted the interest of two rival record companies. Jac Holzman of Elektra Records and Clive Davis of Columbia got into a bidding war to sign him, which Elektra eventually won. His debut album, *Heads and Tales*, contained the single "Taxi"—a story song about a taxi driver meeting up with his old flame—was well-received. The hit was responsible for Chapin's first Grammy nomination for best new artist of 1972.

Chapin quickly produced a follow-up album, *Sniper and Other Love Songs*, which contained the Chapin anthem "Circle," but was not as successful. His third album, *Short Stories* (1973), contained his hit song "W*O*L*D," and his fourth, *Verities and Balderdash* (1974), containing his hit "Cat's in the Cradle," were more successful. "Cat's in the Cradle"—about a father too busy with business to watch his son grow up—brought him a Grammy nomination for best male vocal performance of 1975.

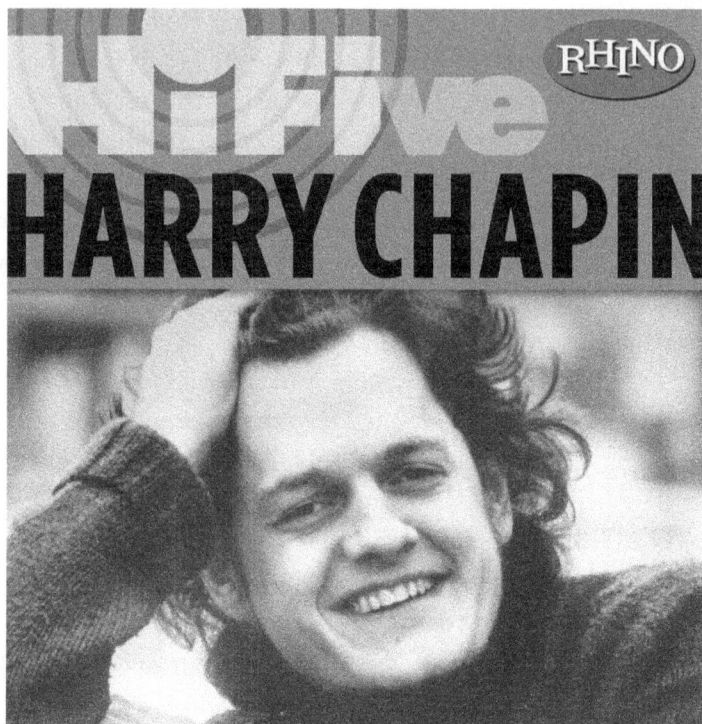

Early Chaplin album cover.

He was performing in concert as much as possible, and his dynamic performance qualities were becoming well-honed. He had become an engaging raconteur, knowledgeable in the making of good drama and good comedy. He routinely received standing ovations and often moved audiences to tears. "There were few dry eyes in the house," wrote *Newsbeat* after a concert at the Bitter End. "It was as powerful a display of emotion and feeling as the Bitter End has rarely seen in a performer." His interaction with his fans was such that during a 1977 appearance at the University of West Florida, when he was touring with only his bass violin player, he recruited the back-up singers for "Mr. Tanner" out of the audience.

While "Cat's in the Cradle" reached number one for two consecutive weeks and remained on the Top 40 charts for 19 weeks, and sold well over a million copies, it was not Harry's favorite. His favorite was "What Made America Famous." The song was based on an actual incident near

1972 Grammy winner Best New Artist.

Harry's home, and Harry thought it one of his best. However, it was seven minutes long and failed to get much play on the radio because of that. Harry loved the song so much; he decided to build a Broadway musical around it. *The Night that Made America Famous* opened at the Ethel Barrymore Theatre on February 26, 1975. The show was nominated for two Tony awards. Chapin also wrote the music and lyrics for the musical *Cotton Patch Gospel*, which opened on Broadway in 1981, after Harry's death. In the early 70s, Harry wrote songs for a children's TV show called *Make a Wish*, which was hosted by his brother Tom. The show won a Peabody in 1971 and an Emmy in 1973. Harry's famous song "Circle" was initially written for *Make a Wish*.

In the mid-1970s, Chapin focused on social activism, mostly raising money to combat hunger in the United States. He saw hunger and poverty as an insult to America. In 1975, he co-founded what was to become his pet project, World Hunger Year (WHY), a charity designed to raise money to fight global famine. On Thanksgiving Day, 1975, he took over New York's WNEW-FM for a 24-hour, commercial-free special devoted to the hunger issue. All-in-all, he gave almost half of his concert proceeds—roughly five million dollars—to causes he felt were worthy.

He contributed personally, but he got others, like Gordon Lightfoot, John Denver, and Kenny Rogers, to do benefits. He continually lobbied

The master of the story song that in at least one case deserved a sequel.

in Washington for hunger causes and was instrumental in President Jimmy Carter's 1978 decision to set up the President's Commission on World Hunger. Robert Redford said of Chapin, "The kind of commitment Harry made is rare. In all my experience in this business, I can honestly say that Harry was the most stand-up guy I ever met."

Harry also released a book of poetry, *Looking . . . Seeing,* in 1975, and sales of his book and concert merchandise were used to support World Hunger Year. In the last six years of his life, Chapin raised more than three million dollars for causes he supported. He made so many appearances for free that, at times, it caused friction with band members, and Harry often performed alone to reduce the costs.

In 1980, Chapin had another big hit with the title track of his last album, *Sequel.* As the title implies, it revisits characters from the story-song "Taxi," ten years later.

Harry Chapin

On July 16, 1981, Chapin was driving in the Long Island Expressway's left lane, on his way to East Meadow, New York, to perform at a free concert, when something went wrong. Near exit 40, in Jericho, he put on his emergency flashers and slowed. He veered into the path of a tractor-trailer, which could not brake in time, and rammed the rear of Chapin's 1975 Volkswagen Rabbit, which burst into flames. By helicopter, he was flown to Nassau County Medical Center, where doctors were unable to revive him. A spokesman for the hospital said Chapin had died of cardiac arrest, and there was no way of knowing if it occurred before or after the accident. Chapin was buried in the Huntington Rural Cemetery in Huntington, New York. His grave is unique, and his epitaph is taken from his song "I Wonder What Would Happen to This World." It reads:

> *Oh, if a man tried*
> *To take his time on Earth*
> *And prove before he died*
> *What one man's life could be worth*
> *I wonder what would happen*
> *To this world.*

At the burial ceremony, Tom and Steve Chapin led the group of friends and family in singing "All My Life's a Circle."

His death was mourned, not only by his fans but also by many of the politicians he had badgered into acting on hunger legislation. Nine Senators and thirty Congressmen rose from the floor of Congress to pay tribute to Chapin.

Harry Chapin once said, "America stands for two things: aiding and abetting the quest of every human being for human rights, human dignity, and human needs; and proving that individuals can make a difference."

On December 7, 1987, on what would have been his 45th birthday, Chapin was posthumously awarded the Congressional Gold Medal for his work on social issues and recognizing him as a key player in the creation of the Presidential Commission on World Hunger (he was the only member who attended every meeting). He was also the inspiration

Tombstone of the man who saw hunger and poverty as an insult to America.

Grave goods left by fans still missing the stories.

for the anti-hunger projects USA for Africa (1985) and Hands Across America (1986), which were organized by Ken Kragen, who had been Chapin's manager at his death. Kragen explained, "I felt like Harry had crawled into my body and was making me do it."

The Harry Chapin Memorial Fund was created in 1981 and is now called the Harry Chapin Foundation. Harry's widow Sandy heads the organization that has its mission to help make a positive difference in communities around the country.

If You Go
If you are in the area, we recommend a stop at Monahan and Fitzgerald Restaurant and Pub in Bayside, New York. It was suggested by this author's cousin, Pat Nash. We had a great time. The food, drinks, service, facility, and hospitality were all great.

6

Porky Chedwick

"The Daddio on the Raddio"

County: Allegheny • Town: Pittsburgh
Buried at Jefferson Memorial Park
401 Curry Hollow Road

Porky Chedwick was a radio pioneer. In the summer of 1948, he began playing "race records" on WHOD AM 860 in Pittsburgh to become one of the first disc jockeys to present racially diverse music in a major American city. He blazed a trail some four years before a more famous Pennsylvania native, Alan Freed, called the music "rock and roll." Chedwick's original playlist comprised old R&B and gospel records he collected over the years. His format of playing old records called "Dusty Discs" was copied by disc jockeys across the country. He is recognized as a founder of the "oldies but goodies" radio format. His radio career spanned 54 years.

George Jacob Chedwick was born on February 4, 1918, in Homestead, Pennsylvania, near Pittsburgh. He was one of ten children to a steelworker father from Lithuania. His mother died when he was young, and Chedwick claimed she gave him the nickname "Porky." Before radio, he went to Munhall High School, delivered newspapers, worked as a sports stringer for the Homestead Daily Messenger, sorted mail for the local post office and called play-by-play sporting events for his alma mater.

His radio career began on August 1, 1948. He responded to an ad seeking on-air talent at a brand new AM radio station, WHOD, in Homestead. His experience in sports writing and his popularity as the local sports announcer got him hired for a ten-minute Saturday sports commentary show. Shortly after, his program was expanded to a half hour, and the sports segment was dropped. His weekly half-hour show

Porky Chedwick

was called *Porky Chedwick's Masterful Rhythm, Blues, and Jazz Show*. The budget for new records was so small he used his personal collection of 78s by black artists. Station managers were amazed by the popularity of his show and expanded his show to five hours, seven days a week.

WHOD was called "The Station of Nations" because of the ethnic mix of immigrant steelworkers they served. It was bought by Dynamic Broadcasting in 1956 and became WAMO, an acronym for the rivers Allegheny, Monongahela, and Ohio. The format became Country and Western, with *The Porky Chedwick Show* the only exception. *Esquire* magazine named Porky "Pittsburgh's favorite DJ." He was given the station's anchor spot from 4 P.M. until sign-off.

During this period, Chedwick developed many nicknames such as the "Pied Piper of Platter," "The Platter Pushing Papa," and the most famous "The Daddio on the Raddio." The suggestion that he was corrupting the youth was largely put to rest when US Senator Estes Kefauver commended him for organizing youth baseball teams to fight juvenile delinquency.

Although payola was the norm then, Porky never took a dime. Money didn't mean much to him. It was said he lived sock hop to sock hop. In the 1960s, he hosted a string of 110 consecutive nightly sock hops. He hosted over 7,000 in his lifetime. A boyhood slingshot accident had cost him an eye, and he didn't drive. He walked many miles carrying records to get to the sockhops. His popularity was legendary. In 1961 to promote the movie *Birdman of Alcatraz,* the Stanley Theater invited Porky to do a live broadcast outside under the marquee. Over 10,000 people were in front of the theater within an hour, and the police estimated 50,000 more were on the way. The resulting traffic jam was enormous. The parkway and streets downtown were bumper to bumper for miles. The traffic jam was so big that Mayor Joseph M Barr personally came to the theater to request an end to the broadcast.

In 1962 *The Porky Chedwick Groove Spectacular* was held at the brand-new civic arena. It was an all-day event headlined by Jackie Wilson and twenty-one other acts, including Bo Diddley, The Flamingos, The Marvelettes, Jerry Butler, The Skyliners, Patty LaBelle, Bobby Vinton, and The Drifters. The arena was sold out, and over 3,000 people were turned away.

In the mid-1980s, radio was changing, and in 1984 WAMO honored him for his years of service and then sacked him. He would work at other Pittsburgh stations until executives from Sheridan Broadcasting (WAMO's parent company) asked him to return in 1992.

In 1991 Porky was diagnosed with a large brain tumor. It sent shock waves throughout Pittsburgh and a national community of artists who felt in his debt. A benefit concert was held at The Syria Mosque to raise funds for an operation. Wolfman Jack emceed the show, including a hall

Chedwick's grave

of fame roster of Doo Wop stars. The tumor was benign, and he received over 5,000 gets well cards while recovering in West Penn Hospital.

On October 19, 1996, Porky was honored at a tribute ceremony at the Rock and Roll Hall of Fame for his contributions as a radio DJ. He is featured in the "Dedicated To the One I Love" exhibit that honors radio DJs. Then again, in 1998, the Hall of Fame honored him with a luncheon for twenty-five Rock and Roll radio pioneers, including Dick Clark, Cousin Brucie, and Casey Kasem.

In August of 1998, a celebration of Porky's 50th anniversary in radio was held at Three Rivers Stadium in Pittsburgh. It was a two-day star-studded show headlined by Little Richard and Bo Diddley.

In 2008 Chedwick and his wife moved to Tarpon Springs, Florida, in August. He missed Pittsburgh and, in 2011, moved back and vowed never to leave again. He resumed broadcasting on internet radio. His last public appearance was six days before his death, at Pittsburgh's fortieth and final Roots of Rock and Roll concert. That show was produced by a longtime friend of this author and Porky Chedwick, Henry J DeLuca.

He died on March 2, 2014, after complaining of chest pains. He walked into the hospital ER under his own power but died shortly after. He was 96.

Media Confidential, a trade magazine, wrote this in his obituary:

Chedwick is given credit by numerous R&B/rock and roll legends, including Bo Diddley, Smokey Robinson, Little Anthony, and myriad others, for giving their recordings their first airplay. Porky Chedwick is responsible for making Pittsburgh, Pennsylvania, "The Oldies Capital of The World" and making the city a testing ground for new R&B from the early '50s through the '70s. The impact of Porky Chedwick's contributions far transcends the boundaries of the Steel City. He never received the notoriety or the paycheck of many DJs who followed in his footsteps; however, his accomplishments are an indelible part of the local and national music and culture.

7

George M. Cohan

"Yankee Doodle Dandy"

County: Bronx • Town: New York
Buried at Woodlawn Cemetery
517 East 233rd Street

George M. Cohan was often referred to as the most significant single figure the American theater has ever produced. He is a Broadway legend and the Father of American Musical Comedy. He was a man of many skills, an actor, singer, dancer, songwriter, playwright, and producer. He is a fiercely patriotic man, probably best known for his World War I songs "Over There" and "You're a Grand Old Flag," for which he received the Congressional Gold Medal from President Franklin D. Roosevelt in 1936.

George Michael Cohan was born in 1878 in Providence, Rhode Island, to Irish Catholic parents. His parents, Helen and Jeremiah, were traveling vaudeville performers who lived out of a trunk and, for the most part, never had a home. The family apparently couldn't resist the publicity value of claiming George was born on the fourth of July, but records indicate that he was born on the third. George and his sister Josephine, who was two years older, were carried along on this nomadic existence and were used in the act. George was used as a prop at first and learned to dance and sing soon after walking and talking. In 1890, George and "Josie" were integrated officially into the act, and the group became The Four Cohans. They would typically tour most of the year and spend summer vacations at his grandmother's home in North Brookfield, Massachusetts. During one of those vacations, George befriended baseball great Connie Mack. He played sandlot baseball, rode his bike, and had many happy summers enjoying ordinary childhood experiences. These

George Cohan

experiences inspired his 1907 musical *50 Miles from Boston*, set in North Brookfield and contains one of his most famous songs, "Harrigan."

Cohan began writing original skits and songs for the family act while in his teens. An important part of Cohan's output of popular songs came from the many stage shows he wrote. As the Four Cohans became increasingly popular, George took on more of the responsibilities for the act, including control of the sketches, songs, and management of the troupe's affairs. The senior Cohan (Jerry) insisted that the Four Cohans were a road act and could never please the hard-nosed critics in New York City. The act traveled to every corner of the United States but bypassed Manhattan year after year. George was frustrated by this, and at age 14, he decided to run off on his own and try to make it on Broadway. Jerry decided to give in and make his debut with his family in the fall of 1893.

They made their Manhattan debut at B.F. Keith's new Union Square Theater, where George's dream turned into a nightmare. Keith was a major vaudeville theater owner, and he needed to fill out the opening bill of his show. To do so, he ordered that the Cohans perform separately. George put up such a fuss that the theater manager almost fired them but instead relegated him to open the show. Audiences typically ignored the first act as they settled in, and George's song and dance were no exception. Josie, however, was a smash hit and became the "toast of New York." George had difficulty finding bookings while Josie was in demand, but he used his time to write songs. Soon he had a string of minor hits, and performers searching for fresh material were seeking out George to write for them. These successful tunes' momentum led Josie to give up solo performing, and the family act was reunited.

George's songs and skits made them more popular than ever, and soon they were earning $1,000 a week. It was around this time that George began ending the shows with what became his trademark: "Ladies and gentlemen, my mother thanks you, my father thanks you, my sister thanks you, and I thank you."

George continued to have a conflict with B.F. Keith, who controlled most of the vaudeville theaters. After one argument, George swore that no Cohan would ever work for Keith again. Thus, the Cohans had no choice but to make the jump to the stage.

While on tour with the family, George met and fell in love with a talented vaudeville singer and comedienne, Ethel Levey. They married in 1899, and although she continued to perform on her own, she frequently joined the Cohans in their shows.

Cohan showcasing a small bit of his amazing talent.

In 1901, George wrote, composed, directed, and produced *The Governor's Son*, his first Broadway production. It was not the hit he hoped for, and poor reviews sent the show packing after 32 performances. Once the show left Broadway, it was a hit, and the Cohans performed it for two profitable years. The same fate awaited his second attempt, *Running for Office*, in 1903.

In 1904, George was introduced to Sam Harris, a gambler and boxing promoter who loved the theater and had a sound business mind. They formed a partnership that took Broadway by storm. Together they put on *Little Johnny Jones*, a patriotic and sentimental production that was the breakout hit for which George had long hoped. George wrote the script and the songs, produced and directed the performance, and starred in the

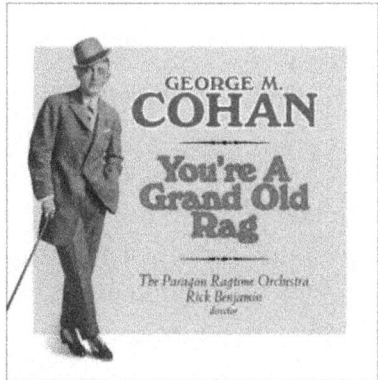

Record cover of the Music of George M. Cohan.

title role. The show introduced two of Cohan's most lasting songs, "Give My Regards to Broadway" and "The Yankee Doodle Boy." The show went on a year-long tour, which included two return trips to New York. Audiences loved him.

In 1906, Cohan wrote a hit show for musical comedy star Fay Templeton called *45 Minutes from Broadway*, and one for the Cohan family called *George Washington, Jr.*, which boasted the wildly popular song "You're a Grand Old Flag," one of the most popular marching band pieces of all-time. George M. Cohan was one of Broadway's top stars, a distinction he relished for the rest of his life.

In 1907, Ethel Levey obtained a divorce from George on the grounds of adultery. She was enormously talented and went on to be one of Broadway's most popular headliners while raising their daughter Georgette on her own. In 1908, George married Agnes Nolan, a chorus girl who had been in some of his shows. The couple would remain married until his death. They had two girls and a boy, all of whom went into show business. Sam Harris married Agnes's sister, and the partners became in-laws.

The Cohan and Harris partnership lasted for 15 years, during which they produced more than 50 shows. At one time, they controlled five theaters in New York and one in Chicago. Cohan's abrasive, demanding business style covered tremendous empathy and generosity to anyone in the theater. He and Harris were unfailingly fair to actors and authors. He was so popular with fellow actors that they made him the "Abbot" of the Friars Club for two terms, a unique honor.

Cohan possessed tremendous energy. He would go on the road as the star of one play, take the cast of another with him, write a script late at night, and rehearse the second cast in the morning. He did most of his writing between midnight and dawn with a pencil on yellow paper. His shows ran simultaneously in as many as five theaters. No one else in the American performing arts has worn so many hats so successfully. An actor and longtime friend William Collier put it this way:

> George is not the best actor or author or composer or dancer or playwright. But he can dance better than any author, compose better than any manager, and manage better than any playwright. And that makes him a very great man.

In 1908, Josie went off on a solo career, and that year *The Yankee Prince* was the last joint appearance by the Four Cohans. In 1916, George suffered the loss of Josie, who died of heart failure, and of his father. He was devastated and threw himself into his work. The next year when the United States entered World War I, Cohan wrote the stirring "Over There," which many say was his greatest hit. It captured the whole nation's attention, and President Woodrow Wilson's secretary sent him a note saying, "The President considers your song 'Over There' a genuine inspiration to all American manhood." In 1918, he toured in a war play called *Out There*, which raised $600,000 for the Red Cross. As the war ended, Cohan seemed to be secure as the King of Broadway, admired by actors, writers, producers, and the general public.

Just after the war, a group of actors banded together to form The Actors' Equity Association. Most producers treated actors very poorly. They often went unpaid, had tours extended or cut without notice, were fired, were forced to rehearse to exhaustion, and even supply their costumes. When producers refused to negotiate with Equity, they called a strike in 1919. Cohan, who was always fair with his actors, surprisingly opposed the strike. He lashed out at Equity in speeches and print and seemed quite surprised when his fellow actors labeled him a traitor. He felt actors were professionals and above unionization. At one point, Cohan proclaimed he would quit acting and run an elevator before giving in to Equity. Comedian Eddie Cantor publicly pointed out that elevator operators were unionized.

With producers losing money and the fall season in jeopardy, Sam Harris led a delegation of producers that agreed to meet Equity's demands. The actors were jubilant. Cohan ended his partnership with Harris, disbanded his production company, quit several theater-centered organizations such as the Friars, and retired for several years. Cohan refused to join the union as an actor, which hampered his ability to appear in his productions. Neither Harris nor Cohan would ever publicly discuss their dispute.

The union granted Cohan a dues-free lifetime membership, but he refused to accept it. Equity actors were allowed to appear with him under an amnesty granted to some members of Equity. For the rest of his life, Cohan was the only actor on Broadway who worked under a non-Equity contract.

In the 1920s, Cohan wrote and produced several successes, such as *The Tavern* and *Little Nellie Kelly*. He continued to announce his retirement every few years but always got drawn back. He had little use for Hollywood and resisted all efforts to get him into films until 1915, when he signed a contract that resulted in three silent films. He did not return to Hollywood until 1932 when he was asked to star in his first talkie, *The Phantom President*. It was a musical and also starred Claudette Colbert and Jimmy Durante. The film got good reviews, but there was friction between Cohan and the producers and directors. He returned to New York, claiming it was his last movie.

He returned to Broadway the next year in Eugene O'Neill's *Ah, Wilderness!* It was in this play that Cohan gave his finest performance as a serious actor. Many were surprised to see the song-and-dance legend in a play by America's most acclaimed modern dramatist, but his performance was so moving that the critics hailed him like never before.

On June 29, 1936, by an act of Congress, Cohan was awarded the Congressional Gold Medal for his contributions to morale during World War I, particularly for the songs "You're a Grand Old Flag" and "Over There." Cohan was the first person in any artistic field selected for this honor. He would keep President Roosevelt waiting to present it until 1940.

In 1937, Cohan played Roosevelt in *I'd Rather Be Right*, which ran for nearly two years. The show was produced by Sam Harris, who remained a close friend and in-law. The show opened amid much hoopla. The critics raved, Roosevelt (a longtime fan) expressed his approval, and the show was a smash.

In 1940, Cohan made one last attempt to produce a Broadway play with *The Return of the Vagabond*. The show closed after only seven performances, and Cohan announced yet another retirement. It was expected that this retirement would prove to be as brief as the others, but Cohan had been diagnosed with terminal stomach cancer, which he kept a secret but never performed again.

In 1941, Warner Brothers produced a film based on Cohan's life. Despite his failing health, he served as a consultant during the production. He approved the choice of James Cagney (see *Gotham Graves Volume One*, Chapter 4), a song and dance man himself early in his career, and was delighted when longtime friend Walter Huston was cast as Jerry Cohan. He lived to see *Yankee Doodle Dandy* become a phenomenal success. The New York premiere on May 20, 1942, raised $5,750,000 worth of war bonds. Mayor Fiorello La Guardia proclaimed July 3, 1942, as "George M. Cohan Day" in New York. Against doctor's orders, Cohan snuck out of his Fifth Avenue apartment in a wheelchair to watch a few minutes of the film at the Hollywood Theater. After hearing the audience cheer his old songs, he had his nurse take him home. It was his last visit to his beloved Broadway.

The film was nominated for eight Academy Awards and won three, including Best Actor for a phenomenal performance by Cagney. In 1993, the film was selected for preservation in the United States National Film Registry by the Library of Congress as "culturally, historically or aesthetically significant."

The remains of the man who gave his regards to Broadway lay within this mausoleum.

George M. Cohan died peacefully in his bedroom on the morning of November 5, 1942, at 64. President Roosevelt telegrammed Mrs. Cohan, saying "a beloved figure is lost to our national life. . . ." After a large funeral at St. Patrick's Cathedral, Cohan was buried at Woodlawn Cemetery in the Bronx, in a private mausoleum he had erected a quarter-century earlier for his sister and his parents. Cohan was always predominantly the artist rather than the businessman. He had an office but rarely went to it. He considered his office to be in his hat and transacted much of his business from public telephone booths.

Cohan's final resting place.

Cohan is remembered in many ways. In 1968, the Broadway musical *George M!* was based on his life. He was inducted into the Songwriters Hall of Fame in 1970, and he received a star on the renowned Hollywood Walk of Fame at 6734 Hollywood Boulevard. The United States Postal Service issued a 15-cent commemorative stamp honoring Cohan on the centenary of his birth, July 3, 1978. There is a bronze bust of him in Providence a few blocks from his birthplace. The city renamed the location the "George M. Cohan Plaza."

In 1956, a memorial committee announced plans for a statue in Cohan's honor to be erected in Times Square. The chairman of the committee was noted songwriter and producer Oscar Hammerstein II. Hammerstein solicited a donation from Actors' Equity for the statue, and the union contributed the cost of lifetime membership, $240. Hammerstein returned the check, claiming he refused to cooperate with pinpricking Cohan's ghost. On September 11, 1959, the statue was unveiled and accepted on behalf of the city by Mayor Robert Wagner at 46th Street and Broadway. The base has an inscription which reads: "Give My Regards to Broadway."

If You Go:

Information about Woodlawn Cemetery can be found in the chapter on Nellie Bly (Chapter 4). The grave of James Cagney, who won an Academy Award playing Cohan in *Yankee Doodle Dandy* and played Cohan again in the 1955 film *The Seven Little Foys*, is located 18 miles from Woodlawn in Gate of Heaven Cemetery in Hawthorne, Westchester County.

8

Michael Constantine

"Gus Portokalos"

County: Berks • Town: Reading
Buried at Charles Evans Cemetery
1119 Centre Avenue

Michael Constantine, from Reading, Pennsylvania, was a highly success-ful actor. His career spanned over six decades, appearing on Broadway, in over thirty Hollywood movies, and in over sixty television shows. Yet despite such a long and prolific career is best known for two roles; first, principal Seymour Kaufman in the TV series *Room 222* (1969–1974), for which he won an Emmy Award and was nominated for a second Emmy and a Golden Globe Award; and second as Gus Portokalos in the smash hit movie *My Big Fat Greek Wedding* (2002). The movie received one Academy Award nomination, two Golden Globe nominations, and many other awards.

Constantine was born Gus Efstratiou in Reading, Pennsylvania, on May 22, 1927. His parents were Greek immigrants, and his father worked as a steelworker. He graduated from Reading High School in 1946 and could sing all four stanzas of the Reading High School alma mater from memory many years later. He loved his hometown and returned there frequently and hung out at bookstores and coffee shops.

After high school and a stint as the manager of the dairy department at a local grocery store, he didn't know what he wanted to do for a living. A chance encounter with a friend who had left Reading for New York to become an actress convinced him to try acting. He studied acting with the legendary Howard DaSilva while supporting himself with odd jobs. He became an understudy to Paul Muni in the role of the character modeled on the famed defense lawyer Clarence Darrow in *Inherit the*

Michael Constantine

Wind. The play opened on Broadway on April 21, 1955, and ran for 806 performances, and won three Tony Awards.

During the run, Constantine managed to work himself also to play the role of Corkin as a replacement. While in the cast, he met and married actress Julianna McCarthy on October 5, 1953. The couple had two children. They divorced in 1969. His next appearance on Broadway was in *Compulsion* in 1957, a dramatization of the Leopold and Loeb trial. It ran for 140 appearances.

In 1959 Constantine was part of the opening night cast of the hit play *The Miracle Worker*. The cast included Anne Bancroft, Patty Duke, and Patricia Neal. It won four Tony Awards. Also, in 1959 he made his big-screen debut in *The Last Mile*, a prison picture starring Mickey Rooney, and followed that in 1961 with a small but memorable supporting role in *The Hustler* starring Paul Newman and Jackie Gleason. That film was nominated for nine Academy Awards.

Around this time, he began appearing as a guest star in TV shows. He made a big impression on five episodes of *The Untouchables* from 1961 to 1963 and appeared in many hit shows such as *Gunsmoke, Perry Mason, The Fugitive, Naked City, Dr. Kildare, The Twilight Zone, Ironsides*, and *The Flying Nun*.

In 1969 Constantine hit it big with a major recurring role in the comedy-drama series *Room 222*. He played Seymour Kaufman, the principal of Walt Whitman High School. Lloyd Haynes, Denise Nicholas, and Karen Valentine also had major roles. In 1970 the show won the Primetime Emmy Award for Outstanding New Series, and Constantine won the Emmy for Outstanding Supporting Actor in a Comedy Series. He was nominated the following year again in the same category. The show lasted until 1974, with 112 episodes on ABC.

After *Room 222*, Constantine stayed busy landing dozens of TV roles on shows such as *Quincy, ME, Roots, The Love Boat, Remington Steele, MacGyver, Murder She Wrote, Magnum PI*, and *Law & Order*, plus more than a dozen films. He was a great character actor, so they turned to him when someone needed one. He was endowed with fierce eyebrows, a personal warmth that belied his hangdog look, and the command of various foreign accents. He played several Jewish characters, Italians, Russians, and even a Greek or two. He was often cast as a lawyer or a tough guy. The former *Reading Eagle* entertainment editor, George Hatza, said it was Constantine's upbringing that made him so adaptable. "He really was the quintessential common man." The family lived the American dream. His parents came to America, and their son grew up to be a TV and movie star.

Despite all this success, he is most famous for his portrayal of Kostas "Gus" Portokalos, the Windex bottle-toting Greek father of Toula Portokalos in the 2002 film *My Big Fat Greek Wedding*. The movie was a surprise international hit that took in more than $360 million and became one of the highest-grossing romantic comedies of all time.

Constantine's grave containing his ashes

Constantine reprised the role first on television in *My Big Fat Greek Life*, a sitcom that appeared briefly on CBS in 2003, and then again on the big screen in *My Big Fat Greek Wedding 2* in 2016.

He died after a long illness on August 31, 2021, at his home in Reading. He was 94 years old. His remains are buried in Charles Evans Cemetery in Reading.

9

Stephen Foster

"The Music Man"

County: Allegheny • Town: Pittsburgh
Buried at Allegheny Cemetery
4734 Butler Street

Who is America's greatest songwriter? Some would say Cole Porter, Irving Berlin, Duke Ellington, or the Gershwins. More recent names like Bob Dylan, Bruce Springsteen, Paul Simon, Smokey Robinson, and Carole King would all find supporters. The first great American songwriter would have to be considered, as well. His name was Stephen Foster, and even today, almost 150 years since his death, his songs are still being performed and recorded.

Stephen Foster was born on July 4, 1826, near Pittsburgh. He was the ninth of ten children born to William and Eliza Foster. The Fosters were a middle-class family. As a boy, Foster was privately tutored, and he also attended private academies in Pittsburgh. From the start, Foster showed more interest in music than in other subjects. In 1839, Foster's older brother, William, had started an apprenticeship as an engineer in Towanda. Foster was placed in William's care, and from 1839 to 1841, he attended Athens Academy. It was here that he composed his first song, "Tioga Waltz," which he performed during the school's 1839 graduation ceremony.

In 1846, Foster moved to Cincinnati, Ohio, where he worked as a bookkeeper for a steamship company. It was in Ohio where Foster composed his first successful songs, including "Oh! Susanna." By 1850 Foster had published the music to twelve songs. That same year, he returned to Pittsburgh, where he married Jane Denny MacDowell. It wasn't until

Stephen Foster

1852 that the couple went on their honeymoon to New Orleans. It was Foster's only trip to the deep South.

By this time, Foster had decided to become a professional composer. He was influenced by Henry Kleber, a German immigrant, who instructed Foster in both composition and songwriting. Foster signed a contract with the Christy Minstrels. The Minstrels were a blackface group formed by the then famous ballad singer Edwin Pearce Christy. The centerpiece of the group's performances became Foster's songs. Foster was writing

OH! SUSANNA.

some of his most famous songs during this period, including "Camptown Races," "My Old Kentucky Home," and "Old Folks at Home," which is also known as "Swanee River." Christy paid Foster $15,000 for the exclusive rights to "Old Folks at Home."

In 1853 Foster moved close to New York to be nearer to his music publishers. His wife joined him a year later. The couple returned to Pittsburgh in the later part of 1854. They lived with Foster's parents for a time, but both his mother and father passed away in 1855. After their deaths, Foster and his wife lived in multiple boarding houses.

Foster's attempt to make a living as a songwriter was unique for the times. Copyright laws regarding music were quite limited. Foster received very little in royalties for most of his work. For example, he was paid $100 for "Oh Susanna." Also, publishers with whom he had no connection would print his songs and pay him nothing. In today's music business, Foster would be making millions.

In 1860 Foster moved back to New York City. His marriage had always been rocky, and a year later, his wife left him and returned to Pittsburgh. By 1863 he began writing songs with George Cooper. Foster supplied the music, and Cooper contributed lyrics designed to appeal to musical theater audiences. Foster's fortunes failed to improve with the new partnership. By 1864 Foster was living in the North American Hotel in the Bowery section of New York. Early that year, he developed a fever that confined him to his bed for several days. He got up to call a chambermaid and fell, hitting the washbasin next to his bed and injuring his head. Foster was taken to the Bellevue Hospital, where he died three days later, on January 13th. He was just 37 years old. His wallet at the time of his death contained 38 cents in Civil War script, three pennies, and a note that read "dear friends and gentle hearts." One of his great works, "Beautiful Dreamer," was published after his death.

In 1970, Foster was inducted into the Songwriters Hall of Fame. He is also a member of the Nashville Songwriters Hall of Fame. "My Old Kentucky Home" is the official state song of Kentucky, and it is sung every year as the horses enter the track at Churchill Downs for the running of the Kentucky Derby. In the 1990s, Bob Dylan recorded the Foster composition "Hard Times" for his album *Good as I've Been to You*. Bruce Springsteen has performed the same song in concert. In 2005, eighteen of Foster's songs were recorded for the album *Beautiful Dreamer: The Songs of Stephen Foster*. The artists who recorded the songs included John Prine, Roger McGuinn, and Allison Krauss. The record won the Grammy for Best Traditional Folk Album.

There are many memorials to Foster. Chief among these is the Stephen Foster Memorial on the campus of the University of Pittsburgh. The building houses the Stephen Foster Memorial Museum, which contains the largest collection of Foster's songs, recordings, and memorabilia. A lake at Mount Pisgah State Park in Pennsylvania is named in his honor. In Cincinnati, there is a statue of Foster overlooking the Ohio River. During the first weekend in July, the Lawrenceville Historical Society and the Allegheny Cemetery Historical Association host the Stephen Foster Music and Heritage Festival appropriately called Doo Dah Days.

If You Go:

Allegheny Cemetery is a historical treasure. Besides Foster, there are many notable interments. The famed singer and actress Lillian Russell was laid to rest here. Hall of Fame baseball player Josh Gibson (see *Keystone Tombstones Volume Two*), who hit 800 home runs in a 17-year career, is buried in

The gravesite of America's first great songwriter.

Allegheny Cemetery. Gibson was a major star in the Negro League, and many who saw him play claimed he was as good if not better than Babe Ruth. Henry Thaw, the man who shot and killed the noted architect Stanford White on the roof of Madison Square Garden, is here as well. The murder is part of the hit movie *Ragtime*. The great jazz saxophonist Stanley Turrentine's final resting place is in Allegheny Cemetery.

Two Civil War Medal of Honor recipients, Archibald H. Rowand Jr. and Alfred L. Pearson, are buried here as well. After the war, Pearson commanded the National Guardsmen who were sent to Luzerne County to quell riots in the Coal Region. He ordered his men to open fire on the rioters and killed several of them. As a result, he was arrested and charged with murder, but a grand jury failed to indict him, and he was set free.

Also, you may want to visit the Arsenal Monument on the cemetery's grounds. The monument honors 43 women buried here after an explosion at the nearby Allegheny Arsenal took their lives. The explosion was the worst industrial accident associated with the Civil War.

Not far from the cemetery, there is a great restaurant called Piccolo Forno. It is located at 3801 Butler Street. The eatery offers great service and terrific Italian food that is very reasonably priced. It's worth checking out.

10

Dave Garroway

"The Communicator"

County: Montgomery • Town: Bala Cynwyd
Buried at West Laurel Hill Cemetery
225 Belmont Avenue

Dave Garroway was a broadcast pioneer. He was the original host of the morning television program *Today* on NBC television. The first show to combine news and entertainment, *Today* was considered a brash experiment when it premiered in 1952.

David Cunningham Garroway was born in Schenectady, New York, on July 13, 1913. His family moved many times before eventually settling in St. Louis, Missouri, when Dave was fourteen. He attended University City High School and Washington University in St. Louis, where he earned a degree in psychology.

After graduation in 1935, Garroway tried his hand as a lab assistant at Harvard, and then as a salesman (selling books initially, and then later piston rings—neither successfully). He decided to take a stab at broadcasting after he made it through the highly competitive interview process to land a position as a page at NBC. The page program gave youn g people a temporary job at Radio City in New York and later the NBC Studios in Hollywood. NBC's pages would work in various departments at the network, being groomed for a career with NBC. Also, the pages acted as ushers and tour guides. Only 60 to 80 pages were selected from thousands of applicants each year, one of whom in 1938 was Dave Garroway.

Garroway got off to a rather mediocre start by graduating 23rd of 24 in his class at the NBC announcer school in 1939. Nevertheless, he landed a job at influential Pittsburgh radio station KDKA and built a reputation

Dave Garroway, "Peace."

as the station's "Roving Announcer." He roamed the region, filing several memorable reports from both above and below the Earth's surface (aboard a hot-air balloon and from deep within a coal mine, respectively) as well as underwater (aboard a U.S. Navy submarine in the Ohio River). This experience brought out Garroway's ability to find a compelling story in any situation. He soon became the station's special events director.

After two years at KDKA, Garroway left Pittsburgh for a job in Chicago. However, his career in broadcasting was interrupted in 1941 by the outbreak of World War II. He enlisted in the Navy and was stationed in Honolulu. When he was off duty, he hosted a radio show, playing jazz and reminiscing about Chicago.

After the war, he returned to Chicago and worked as a disc jockey at WMAQ (AM). He hosted a variety of programs and promoted the Chicago jazz scene. One of his innovations was to convince his studio audience to show approval for a song by snapping their fingers instead of clapping, just like the "hepcats" did in the coffee shops. He was voted the nation's best disc jockey in the Billboard polls in 1948, 1949, and 1951.

Garroway broke into television when he hosted the experimental musical variety show *Garroway at Large*, which was telecast live from Chicago. The show ran from 1949 to 1954 on NBC. He abandoned the usual conventions for a more casual approach and personal, informal style. In 1951, he came to the attention of legendary NBC president Pat Weaver, who recruited Garroway to host a new morning news-and-entertainment experiment called the *Today* show. The show debuted on January 14, 1952, and the critics initially panned it, but Garroway's laid-back style attracted a large audience that enjoyed his easygoing presence early in the morning.

On *Today*, Garroway—who wore bowties and horn-rimmed glasses—was officially called "a communicator," and his former colleagues say the term was especially apt. His signature sign-off at the end of each broadcast was an upraised hand (palm out) saying "Peace." Barbara Walters, who Garroway hired to be a writer on *Today*, said of Garroway, "I have never seen anyone in this business who could communicate the way he could. He could look at the camera and make you feel that he was talking only with you."

Garroway's co-host was a cute chimpanzee named J. Fred Muggs, and Garroway took the show to Paris and Rome, to car shows and expos, to plays and movies, and even onboard an Air Force B-52 for a practice bombing run.

Garroway was a hard worker. At the same time, he did *Today*, he hosted a Friday night variety series called *The Dave Garroway Show*, which ran from 1953 to June 1954. In 1955, he began hosting NBC's Sunday afternoon live documentary, *Wide Wide World*, which ran until 1958. The premiere episode—featuring entertainment from the U.S., Canada, and

Mexico—was the first international North American telecast in the history of the medium. He also hosted a radio show, *Dial Dave Garroway*, that went on air as soon as the *Today* show wrapped up each morning, and for those who couldn't get enough of him, there was a board game called Dave Garroway's Today Game, which debuted in 1960.

Despite his easygoing camera presence, Garroway frequently battled depression. After his second wife, Pamela Wilde, committed suicide via drug overdose in April 1961, his condition worsened. A month later, he resigned, and on June 16, 1961, he hosted his last *Today*.

After leaving the show, Garroway tried his hand at educational television (a series called *Exploring the Universe*), a return to radio, and even started a magazine. He studied acting (landing a role in an episode of the western series *Alias Smith and Jones* in 1972), narrated a compilation of songs performed by the Boston Pops Orchestra, and wrote a book (*Fun on Wheels*) to amuse children on road trips. He appeared sporadically on various television programs but never again achieved the success or recognition he enjoyed on *Today*. He appeared on *Today* anniversary shows in the '60s and '70s; his final appearance was on the 30th-anniversary show on January 14, 1982.

He had many interests and hobbies, such as restoring classic cars, astronomy, music, and auto racing. He appeared in television commercials for the first Corvette in 1953 and the Ford Falcon in 1964. His interest in astronomy led him to his third wife, Sarah Lee Lippincott, an astronomer whom he married in 1980.

In 1982, Dave Garroway had open-heart surgery. Various postoperative complications soon followed. On July 21, 1982, he was found dead of a self-inflicted gunshot wound at his home in Swarthmore, Pennsylvania. He was 69 years old.

The Hollywood Walk of Fame honored Dave Garroway with a star at 6264 Hollywood Boulevard for his contributions to television, and another, separate star at 6355 Hollywood Boulevard for his contributions to radio. Because of his dedication to the cause of mental health, his third wife, Sarah, helped establish the Dave Garroway Laboratory for the Study of Depression at the University of Pennsylvania. He is buried in West Laurel Hill Cemetery in Bala Cynwyd.

Here is the grave of the broacast pioneer Dave Garroway.

If You Go:

West Laurel Hill is a beautiful, large cemetery containing the graves of many famous and interesting people, including:

William Breyer (1828–1882), the founder of Breyer's Ice Cream;

Hobart "Hobey" Baker (1892–1918), the Hall-of-Fame hockey player and World War I hero;

Robert Cooper Grier (1794–1870), a United States Supreme Court Justice, Grier was plucked from relative obscurity in August 1846 and nominated for appointment to the nation's highest bench by President James K. Polk, but not until after one of Polk's first nominees (fellow Pennsylvanian and future President of the United States, James Buchanan) refused the appointment; and

Herman Haupt (1817–1904), a very important Civil War general (*see Keystone Tombstones: The Civil War*).

See the "If You Go" section of Chapter 18 in Volume One for more notable people.

11

George and Ira Gershwin

"The Gershwin Brothers"

County: Westchester • Town: Hastings on Hudson
Westchester Hills Cemetery
400 Saw Mill River Road

Brothers George and Ira Gershwin composed some of the most memorable songs of the Twentieth Century. They are responsible for hit songs like "Someone to Watch Over Me," "Summertime," "I Got Rhythm," "Rhapsody in Blue," "They Can't Take That Away From Me," and for such musicals as *Funny Face* and the first musical ever to win a Pulitzer Prize, *Porgy and Bess*.

The brothers Ira (born in 1896) and George (born in 1898) were the oldest of four children born to Morris and Rose Gershowitz. Sometime in the 1890s, Morris changed his surname to Gershwine, and, around that time, moved the family to a dwelling on Snediker Avenue in Brooklyn, where George was born. George changed the name to Gershwin after becoming a professional musician, and other family members followed suit.

The boys grew up around the Yiddish Theater District and frequented the local Yiddish theaters, with George occasionally appearing onstage as an extra. The parents bought a piano for lessons for Ira, but it was George who took to it. He tried various piano teachers before finally settling on Charles Hambitzer, who became George's musical mentor.

In 1913, at the age of fifteen, George quit school to study music and began composing. By 1916, George was "plugging" in the Tin Pan Alley. "Song pluggers" were pianists and singers who made their living demonstrating songs to promote sheet music sales. He worked as a plugger for

George Gershwin

Jerome H. Remick and Company, a Detroit-based publishing firm, for which he was paid fifteen dollars a week.

George's first published song was "When You Want 'Em, You Can't Get 'Em, When You've Got 'Em, You Don't Want 'Em." He was seventeen at the time and received fifty cents for the song. In 1919, he had his first big hit, "Swanee," which Al Jolson popularized, and his first Broadway show, *La La Lucille*. The song was written as a big production number for a New York revue called *Demi-Tasse*, with Irving Caesar writing the

Ira Gershwin

lyrics. The song had little impact in its first show, but Gershwin played it at a party where Jolson heard it. Jolson put it in his show *Sinbad* and recorded it for Columbia Records. The song went to number one. A million sheet music copies of the song, and an estimated two million records, were sold. It was George's first hit and became the biggest selling song of his career. The money he saved from it allowed him to concentrate on theater work and films rather than writing single pop hits.

During this time, George's brother Ira worked as a cashier in his father's Turkish baths. It was not until 1921 that Ira became involved in the music business. George had been encouraging Ira to write lyrics, and he did write some songs using the pen name Arthur Francis. His first published song was "You May Throw All the Rice You Desire but Please Friends, Throw No Shoes."

In 1921, Ira was asked to write the lyrics for the show *Two Little Girls in Blue*. He did, and the show was critically acclaimed. In 1924, the brothers teamed up to write the music for their first hit show, *Lady Be Good*. Ira dropped his pen name, and the next decade of collaboration would cement the brothers firmly in American musical history. They became one of the most influential forces in the history of American musical theater. Together, they wrote the music for more than a dozen shows and four films. Some of their more famous works include "I Got Rhythm," "Someone to Watch Over Me," "They Can't Take That Away From Me," and "Fascinating Rhythm."

In 1928, the Gershwins went on a trip to Europe, and that trip is said to have inspired the iconic *An American in Paris*. It got mixed reviews upon its first performance at Carnegie Hall on December 13, 1928, but quickly became a smash hit in the U.S. and Europe. In 1931, the Gershwins wrote the music for the hit musical *Of Thee I Sing*, which became the first musical to win the Pulitzer Prize for Drama.

The Gershwin brothers' biggest triumph came in 1935, with their famous folk opera, *Porgy and Bess*. The characters in the musical were almost exclusively African American. The Gershwins insisted on hiring only black singers to play the parts, a progressive move when blackface entertainment—white actors with their faces painted to resemble black people—was still common.

Porgy and Bess contains some of the Gershwins' most sophisticated music, combining elements of popular music of the day with a strong influence of African-American music of the period and techniques typical of opera. Some of the set numbers like "Summertime," "I Got Plenty O' Nuttin'," and "It Ain't Necessarily So" are of the most refined and ingenious of George's compositions. Initially, a commercial failure in the middle of the Great Depression, *Porgy and Bess* has since been recognized as one of the greatest musicals and theatrical compositions of the Twentieth Century. It was revived on Broadway in 1942, and in 1952, a production of the show toured Europe and North America to rave reviews. The cast of the 1952 production included Leontyne Price, Cab Calloway, and Maya Angelou.

George Gershwin, one of the greatest composers of the 20th century.

In 1959, a film version of *Porgy and Bess* was produced by Sam Goldwyn and directed by Otto Preminger. The movie starred Sidney Poitier, Diahann Carroll, Sammy Davis, Jr., Dorothy Dandridge, and Pearl Bailey. André Previn's adaptation of the score won him an Academy Award.

After the commercial failure of *Porgy and Bess*, the Gershwins moved to Hollywood to write the music for the film *Shall We Dance*, starring Fred Astaire and Ginger Rogers. The song "They Can't Take That Away from Me" from the movie was nominated for an Academy Award.

Early in 1937, George complained of blinding headaches and a recurring impression that he smelled burning rubber. In February, he suffered coordination problems and blackouts during his music performance with the San Francisco Symphony. As the headaches and olfactory hallucinations continued, he began to exhibit mood swings and irrational behavior. He was admitted to Cedars of Lebanon Hospital in Los Angeles, but tests showed no physical cause, and he was released with a diagnosis of "likely hysteria." Two weeks later, he collapsed and was rushed back to the hospital, where he fell into a coma. Only then did the doctors deter

Two talented brothers.

mine he was suffering from a brain tumor. His condition was judged to be critical, and the doctors performed emergency surgery, but it proved unsuccessful. George Gershwin died on the morning of July 11, 1937, at the age of 38. He was interred at Westchester Hills Cemetery.

George's many friends and fans were devastated. His brother Ira waited nearly three years before writing again, working with composer Kurt Weill, Jerome Kern, and Harold Arlen. The 1946 production of *Park Avenue*, a flop, was Ira's last work for Broadway. In 1947, he took eleven songs George had written but never used, provided them with new lyrics, and put them into Betty Grable's film *The Shocking Miss Pilgrim*. His final major work was for the 1954 Judy Garland film *A Star Is Born*.

In 1959, Ira released an album of his work, *Lyrics on Several Occasions*, and finally retired in 1960, after more than 30 years of songwriting. He spent the rest of his life working on the family archive with musical

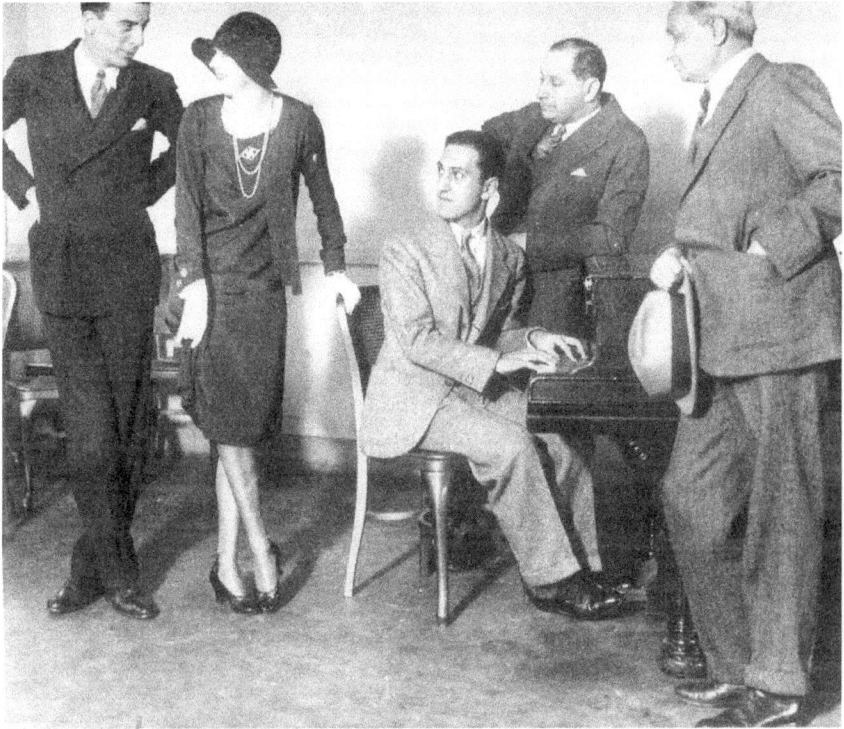

George Gershwin at the center of the action.

historian Michael Feinstein. Ira Gershwin died in Beverly Hills on August 17, 1983, at the age of 86. He was interred with his brother.

The contributions of the Gershwins are memorialized in many ways. In 2007, the United States Library of Congress named its Prize for Popular Song after them. The prize is given annually to a composer or performer whose contributions exemplify the standard of excellence associated with the Gershwins. The Gershwin Room at the Library of Congress has George's piano and Ira's typewriter on display.

The Congressional Gold Medal was awarded to George and Ira Gershwin in 1985. Only three other songwriters—George M. Cohan (see Chapter 7), Harry Chapin (see Chapter 5), and Irving Berlin (see *Gotham Graves Volume Two*, Chapter 1)—have won this award.

A special Pulitzer Prize was posthumously awarded to the Gershwins, in 1998, for their enduring contributions to American music. The

Final resting place of the Gershwin brothers who were awarded the Congressional Gold Medal in 1985.

Gershwin Theatre, on Broadway, is named in their honor, and they have a star on the Hollywood Walk of Fame at 7083 Hollywood Boulevard.

If You Go

Westchester Hills is a Jewish cemetery and contains the graves of many noteworthy people. One of the most famous is John Garfield (1913–1952, age 39). Garfield was a major movie star for Warner Brothers in the 1930s and 1940s. He is most remembered for his role opposite Lana Turner in *The Postman Always Rings Twice* (1946). Garfield was nominated for the Academy Award for Best Supporting Actor for *Four Daughters* in 1939 and Best Actor for *Body and Soul* in 1948. His life and career ended tragically. He was a target of the House Un-American Activities Committee during its investigation of Communists in the entertainment industry. When asked at a Committee hearing to identify Communist party members or followers, Garfield refused to name names and, in fact, testified he knew of none in the film industry.

Nevertheless, his career was shattered. Garfield was blacklisted and barred from employment by Hollywood movie bosses. On May 21,

Gershwin mausoleum located in the Westchester Hills Cemetery.

1952, he died of heart problems allegedly aggravated by the stress of his blacklisting. Garfield has a star on the Hollywood Walk of Fame, at 7065 Hollywood Boulevard, a short distance from the Gershwins' star.

Tony Randall (1920–2004, age 84), a highly respected and accomplished stage actor, is also buried at Westchester Hills. He was born Leonard Rosenberg in Tulsa, Oklahoma, and served in the Army Signal Corps in World War II. He made a name for himself on Broadway in the 1950s, where he was popular in numerous Broadway plays. He also found success in television and was nominated for an Emmy for his role as Wally Cox's sidekick in *Mr. Peepers* (1952–1953). Many remember him for his portrayal of neat-freak Felix Unger, opposite sloppy roommate Oscar Madison (played by Jack Klugman) in *The Odd Couple*, which premiered on ABC in 1970, and ran for five seasons. Randall had two children, becoming a first-time father at the age of 77, when his second wife—50 years his junior—gave birth to a daughter, followed by a son a year later.

Actor, director, and acting teacher Lee Strasberg (1901–1982, age 80) is also buried at Westchester Hills. In 1951, he became director of the non-profit Actors' Studio in New York City, considered the nation's most prestigious acting school. He is considered the father of method acting in America, having trained several generations of notable actors, including Ann Bancroft (see *Gotham Gravestones Volume One*, Chapter 2), Dustin Hoffman, Paul Newman, Jane Fonda, Robert DeNiro, James Dean, Marilyn Monroe, and Al Pacino. As an actor, Strasberg is probably best known for his role as gangster Hyman Roth in *The Godfather-Part II*. Strasberg took the role at Pacino's suggestion, and his performance earned him an Academy Award nomination for Best Supporting Actor (1974). He died of a heart attack, in 1982, at the age of 80. He, too, has a star on the Hollywood Walk of Fame.

Also interred at Westchester Hills is David Susskind (1920–1987, age 66), an Emmy-award winning producer of television, movies, and stage plays. He was also a pioneer TV talk show host. *The David Susskind Show* ran from 1958 to 1986, covering all the issues of the time and featuring a wide-ranging guest list for nearly three decades. He died of natural causes in February 1987, six months after his show was canceled and went off the air.

13

Charles Grodin

"The Heartbreak Kid"

County: Allegheny • Town: Allison Park
Buried in Adath Jeshurun Cemetery
4779 Roland Road

Charles Grodin was a successful actor on both stage and screen, writer, comedian, author, talk show host, and political commentator. He was talented, smart, handsome, articulate, and popular, yet success didn't come easy. Show business is hard for most people, and as Grodin said, "Maybe the only way harder than show business to make a living is selling poetry door to door."

He was born in Pittsburgh on April 21, 1935, to Orthodox Jewish parents. His father, Theodore, owned a store that sold wholesale supplies to cleaners, tailors, and dressmakers. His grandfather Charles had changed the family name from Grodinsky to Grodin. His mother, Lena, kept house and worked in the family business. He had a brother Jack who was six years older and became a very successful lawyer and CPA.

He graduated from Peabody High School as valedictorian and was known for asking many questions. Peabody had elections for class officers twice a year, and Chuck Grodin was elected class president eight times. He wasn't in school plays because he had to work after school in his father's store and wasn't available for rehearsals. After graduating, he had no strong ideas about what to do and figured he'd study journalism at the University of Pittsburgh. Then he saw the movie *A Place in The Sun* with Montgomery Clift and Elizabeth Taylor and decided he wanted to be an actor. He decided he wanted to major in drama at the University of Miami. His father strongly opposed the idea and felt it

Charles Grodin

was a disastrous choice. Even so, he agreed to support his son's passion and pay for Chuck to go. Then before Chuck left for school, his father suddenly died. He left two months later for Miami but was still grieving and depressed over his loss. He dearly loved his father. Still depressed and homesick at the Christmas break, he auditioned for a scholarship at the Pittsburgh Playhouse and got it. He was awarded the scholarship by Bill Putch, who was later to marry Jean Stapleton. He graduated from the Pittsburgh Playhouse, although he was disappointed in the overall experience. However, he enjoyed two summers of summer stock at The Little Lake Theater in nearby Canonsburg, Pennsylvania.

After his second season at Little Lake Theater, Grodin decided to go to Hollywood in search of his dream. After a heavy dose of rejection and disinterest, he decided he had made a mistake and should go to New York for more study. He applied to study in the Actor's Studio with Lee Strasberg but was rejected. He then got an audition with Uta Hagen, who was one of the most respected actresses and teachers in New York. She accepted him into her beginner's class. He attended classes with Uta for the next three years while trying to find work as an actor. He drove a cab and worked as a night watchman and then managed to get accepted to study with Lee Strasberg at the Actor's Studio.

After six years in New York, he got his first audition for a Broadway show and got the part. The play was *Tchin-Tchin,* and it starred Anthony Quinn and Margaret Leighton. It garnered four Tony nominations and ran for 225 performances.

On screen, Grodin received his first big break with a minor role in the cult favorite 1968 horror film *Rosemary's Baby.* In 1964 he landed a role in the ABC soap opera *The Young Marrieds,* where he played Matt Stevens. The show ran for 65 episodes.

Grodin was offered the part of Benjamin Braddock in *The Graduate* but turned it down because of the low salary offered by the producer Lawrence Turman. Turman assured him the part would make him a star, as it did only for Dustin Hoffman. While licking his wounds, he was asked to direct a Broadway play called *Lovers and Other Strangers.* It got rave reviews and later was made into a successful movie.

Ironically he landed a supporting role in the movie *Catch 22;* the irony being that Mike Nichols was directing, and he also directed *The Graduate.* The movie was a big success and did Grodin's career much good. During the filming, he forged a friendship with Art Garfunkel. Through Garfunkel, he met Paul Simon, which led to a remarkable experience. They asked him to direct their special *Songs of America.* The show contained footage of Simon and Garfunkel on stage, in the studio, and on tour across America. It had footage of Cesar Chavez, Martin Luther King, John and Robert Kennedy and made many anti-Vietnam War references. The show's original sponsor, AT&T, dropped out of its sponsorship after seeing a preview. They found another sponsor, and the show was a critical success but never aired again. Later in 1978, Grodin won several awards, including the Primetime Emmy Award for Outstanding Writing for the Paul Simon special.

During the late '60s, the versatile Grodin appeared in many television shows such as *The FBI*, *The Virginian*, *Felony Squad*, and *Judd for the Defense*. In 1972 he hit it big with his performance in the movie *The Heartbreak Kid*, for which he received a Golden Globe nomination. The movie was a critical and commercial success, and "suddenly after seventeen years, I was considered a movie star," Grodin quipped.

He followed that up by starring opposite Ellen Burstyn in the smash Broadway hit *Same Time Next Year*. The play won three Tony Awards, but Grodin was not nominated. Burstyn was and felt bad that Grodin had been slighted. "Not being nominated for an award wasn't very high on my list of bad things that could happen to you," he remarked.

He finished up the '70s doing a string of hit movies such as *King Kong*, *Heaven Can Wait*, and *Real Life*, and he both starred in and wrote the screenplay for *11 Harrowhouse*.

He started the '80s with *The Great Muppet Caper* and *Seems Like Old Times* and finished with perhaps his greatest performance in the hit comedy *Midnight Run*, co-starring Robert De Niro. The film received Golden Globe nominations for Best Picture and Best Actor for De Niro. In an interview, De Niro attributed the film's success to Grodin.

Grodin also wrote several plays that saw New York stage production, including *The Price of Fame*, *One of the All-Time Greats*, and *The Right Kind of People*.

In the mid-90s, he took a twelve-year hiatus from film to be more present for his family. From 1995 through 1998, he hosted his own issue-oriented talk show on CNBC called *The Charles Grodin Show*; in 2000, he became a political commentator for *60 Minutes II*.

What made Grodin so special and unique is that you never really knew whether his curmudgeon act was an act. He belonged to the Bob Newhart school of wry comedy that values understatement and subtlety. Clearly, he was a lot more than just a comic actor.

He hosted *Saturday Night Live*, where the entire show revolved around his forgetting the show was live and being unprepared for each sketch. He appeared on *Late Night with David Letterman* 17 times. He returned to film in 2006, acting in the comedy *The Ex*, starring Zach

Braff. That same year he received the William Kunstler Award for Racial Justice.

His last screen credit was for the ABC miniseries *Madoff* in 2016. He died on May 18, 2021, at home of multiple myeloma. He was 86.

Grave of Grodin's parents in Pittsburgh

12

Billie Holiday

"Lady Day"

County: Bronx • Town: New York
Buried at Saint Raymond's Cemetery
2600 Lafayette Avenue

She was born in Philadelphia but spent her formative years in Baltimore and New York. It was in New York that she began her show business career. While still in her teens, she started performing in Harlem clubs, going from table to table, singing for tips. Here she came to the attention of a young record producer named John Hammond (who would later sign Bob Dylan and Bruce Springsteen to their first recording contracts). With Hammond's backing, she recorded her first record at the age of 18. Her distinctive vocal style earned her a reputation as a seminal influence on both jazz and pop singing. Barbara Streisand has stated, "If I hear a record once, I usually never listen to it again. I rarely listen to music—unless it's Billie Holiday."

According to her birth certificate, Holiday was born on April 7, 1915, in Philadelphia and named Elinore Fagan. However, the hospital records show Eleanor, and she said her birth name was Eleanora. Her teenaged parents, Sarah Fagan and Clarence Holiday, were not married, nor did they live together. Her father left mother and daughter behind to become a jazz guitarist. Though Holiday is commonly acknowledged to be the father, the aforementioned birth certificate identifies the father as Frank DeViese. It is a fact that the elder Holiday never publicly stated that he was Billie Holiday's father until she became well known and successful.

Details of Holiday's childhood are sketchy at best. In Baltimore, it appears that she was living with and raised by her mother's half-sister. While being shuttled between relatives, Holiday was at worst abused and

Billie Holiday

at best neglected. The possibility exists that she may have been raped during this period. The youngster frequently skipped school, and in 1925, she found herself in juvenile court at the age of nine as a result of truancy. The court sent her to a Catholic reform school where she spent nine months before being released to her mother's care. By the time she was eleven, Holiday had dropped out of school.

Holiday's mother had started a relationship with Wee Wee Hill, a porter she had met while working in the transportation industry. Leaving the girl behind with her half-sister, the couple moved to Harlem, New York. Once the two separated in 1929, Holiday joined her mother, living and working in a Harlem brothel. Holiday, who had yet to reach the age of 14, also became a prostitute. Mother and daughter were both arrested during a police raid in May of 1929. After serving some time in a workhouse, Holiday was released the following October.

Back in Harlem, Holiday began singing in multiple nightclubs. She took the name Billie from an actress and Holiday from her father. Her reputation around Harlem began to grow, and by 1932, she was the leading singer at a club called Covan's. It was during a performance here that John Hammond first heard her perform. Years later, Hammond was asked what it was about Billie Holiday that got his attention. Hammond responded by saying he heard a singer who sounded like an improvising horn player and never sang a song the same way twice. Hammond recalled that he had to be sold on Holiday because he turned down the chance to work with Ella Fitzgerald to concentrate on Holiday.

Through Hammond, Holiday began working with some of the really big names in the music business. Her first recordings were made with Benny Goodman. When she was 18, she appeared in a short film *Symphony in Black* with Duke Ellington. She then began working with the noted jazz pianist Teddy Wilson. The two would take standard pop tunes like "Yankee Doodle" and work their jazz magic on them. Today the recordings made by Holiday and Wilson back in the 1930s are considered classics. Together they recorded more than ninety songs.

In 1937, Holiday took to the road as a big band vocalist with Count Basie. They were booked to play at the Fox Theater in Detroit. The management felt that her skin tone wasn't dark enough to sing with Basie's black band, so they applied makeup to blacken her face. Holiday went on but later recalled, "I had to be darkened so the show could go on in dynamic-asset Detroit. There's no damn business like show business. You have to smile to keep from throwing up."

Basie's saxophonist was the talented Lester Young, and he and Holiday hit it off perfectly. The two would eventually make 49 recordings. Though they teamed on fantastic songs like "Foolin' Myself" and "Easy Living," Young would pick "A Sailboat in the Moonlight" as his favorite piece. Some describe the song by saying that within it, the vocal and the saxophone become one. The two were so close that they gave each other nicknames that stuck; she called him "Pres," and he christened her "Lady Day."

By all accounts, Holiday's short stint with Basie's band was a rocky experience, and she was eventually fired. From her account, she was upset over her wages and the working conditions. Basie's male vocalist said she was unprofessional. The official word was that she was let go for being temperamental and unreliable. It appears that these reports didn't scare off Artie Shaw, who hired her to sing with his band within a month.

Working with Shaw certainly widened her audience. She was among the first black women hired to perform with a white orchestra. This caused some problems when Shaw decided to take his band on a Southern tour. In her autobiography, Holiday tells of not being allowed to perform on the same stage as the other vocalists because of her race. She recalled that Shaw, ignoring the rule, told her to get up here with the band. However, it was a racial incident in New York City that may have caused Holiday to leave Shaw. The band played the Lincoln Hotel, and Holiday was told to use the service elevator after the hotel manager received complaints from white patrons. She was also not permitted to enter the bar or the dining areas though the other band members faced no such prohibition. In addition to the racial slights, she was also upset with the number of songs Shaw was permitting her to perform, so she left the band.

By this time, her recordings for Columbia records had made her an established star. Yet Columbia refused to record the song with which she is most closely associated. She is said to have first performed the song in 1939, at the Cafe Society in New York's Greenwich Village. This was a progressively integrated nightclub that catered to the liberal mindset. Yet even in this setting, Holiday was reluctant to sing the song and did so only after being prodded by Barney Jacobson, the club owner.

Lady sings the blues.

Holiday would recall after the initial performance, the song was met with a stunned silence that was only broken when one person in the audience began to applaud. The rest of the crowd joined in, and the song became her signature piece. It was written by a white Jewish schoolteacher, Abel Meeropol, titled "Strange Fruit."

The song was a protest song written before such a label existed. It focused on American racism, specifically the lynching of black Americans. In the first verse, Holiday sings:

> Southern trees bear strange fruit,
> Blood on the leaves and blood on the root,
> Black body swinging in the southern breeze,
> Strange fruit hanging from the poplar trees.

Columbia, feeling that the song was too controversial and fearing a backlash from Southern record retailers, refused to record it. Holiday was granted a one-session release from her Columbia contract to record the song for Commodore records. That recording became her best-selling record. Ahmet Ertegun, the founder of Atlantic Records, called "Strange Fruit" the beginning of the civil rights movement. In 1978, Holiday's version was inducted into the Grammy Hall of Fame. In 1999, *Time* magazine declared that "Strange Fruit" was the song of the century, and in 2002 the Library of Congress added the tune to the National Recording Registry.

In 1941, Holiday and pianist Arthur Herzog wrote and recorded "God Bless the Child." The record sold over a million copies and was named number three by Billboard when they ranked the year's songs. Holiday said that the song's title came from an argument that she had with her mother that ended with her yelling, "God bless the child that's got his own."

Holiday was quoted as saying, "Somebody once said we never know what is enough until we know what's more than enough." Certainly, that was the way she lived her life. She started smoking tobacco when she was fifteen, and in time she'd be smoking 50 cigarettes a day, not including the marijuana she freely ingested. She also drank heavily and seemed to be attracted to men who abused her. In 1941, she married James Monroe, and though the union didn't last, he introduced Holiday to opium. Her next marriage to trumpeter Joe Guy was short-lived, but he did introduce her to heroin. She became addicted to the latter drug, and on May 16, 1947, she was arrested in New York for possession of narcotics.

One year earlier, Holiday had made her only featured film, *New Orleans,* which also starred Louis Armstrong (see *Gotham Graves Volume One,* Chapter 1). Holiday was upset that many of her musical numbers ended up on the cutting room floor, but truth be told, her drug addictions were a significant problem during the filming. Joe Guy, who was supplying her with drugs, had to be banned from the set.

As a result of her arrest, Holiday was sentenced to a year and a day in prison. She served eight months before being released because of good behavior. Though she had served her time, her conviction continued to haunt her. As a felon, she could no longer obtain a cabaret card, which meant that she could no longer work in New York nightclubs. Finding work outside of Gotham grew difficult as well since club owners were reluctant to hire her because of her reputation as an addict as well as her unreliability. Her recording sales plummeted, as did the radio play of her recordings. One reviewer writing in *Downbeat* said that she was becoming "Lady Yesterday."

In 1948, John Levy, owner of the Ebony Club, booked her to perform at his New York club even though it was illegal. Levy would become her boyfriend and her manager. Like the previous men in her life, he was physically abusive. Her performance at the club went on uninterrupted and was judged to be a success. However, as Levy hoped it would, it did not result in Holiday regaining her cabaret card.

At this point, her life might be best summed up in the lyrics of a song she recorded and often performed live. The 1920s blues standard titled "Ain't Nobody's Business if I Do" concludes with this final verse:

> Well, I'd rather my man would hit me
> Then follow him to jump up and quit me
> Ain't nobody's business if I do.
> I swear I won't call no copper, if I'm beat up by my papa
> Ain't nobody's business if I do.

Holiday had made a good deal of money but had lost most of it to drugs. By the 1950s, the drinking, drugs, and abusive relationships caught up to her and took their toll on her health. Her voice had changed some say for the worst. The quality of the recordings she made during this period continues to be debated by jazz fans. Miles Davis was not among those who felt that Holiday had lost it. In 1958 he said, "You know she's not thinking now what she was in 1937, and she's probably learned more about different things. And she still has control, probably more control than then. No, I don't think she's in decline."

During the '50s, Holiday kept busy as she toured Europe and began recording for Verve records. In 1956, her autobiography, *Lady Sings the Blues*, was published. William Duffy ghostwrote the book, and it was based on conversations the writer had with the singer. Later, when asked about some of the information in the account of her life story, Holiday claimed, "I ain't never read that book."

In that same year, Holiday performed two concerts to sold-out audiences at Carnegie Hall. The following year she appeared on the television show, *The Sound of Jazz*, where she sang a song she had written called "Fine and Mellow." She was reunited with Lester Young on the show, and their performance has been called the most moving jazz moment ever captured on film. The clip is available on YouTube, and it is indeed brilliant.

Holiday married again in 1957. The groom was Louis McKay, a mafia enforcer, who like the previous men in her life, was abusive, but unlike those who had gone before him, he tried to get her off drugs. He was unsuccessful.

Maya Angelou had a memorable meeting with Holiday around this time that she described in her book *The Heart of a Woman*. Angelou was a calypso singer, and her voice coach brought Holiday to her home in Los Angeles. For five straight days, Holiday visited Angelou. On the fifth day, Holiday accompanied Angelou to watch her perform. With Holiday seated in the front row, Angelou began singing her first song only to be interrupted by Holiday yelling, "Stop that bitch. Stop her goddamit. Stop that bitch. She sounds just like my goddam mamma." Holiday then rose and headed for the women's bathroom with Angelou in pursuit. Once in the bathroom, Angelou said, "Billie, let me tell you something . . ." But that was as far as she got before Holiday interrupted her telling her not to worry about the song since she couldn't help how she sounded. After a very short conversation, Holiday said, "You want to be famous, don't you?" Angelou admitted that she did. Holiday responded, "You're going to be famous. But it won't be for singing."

Early in 1959, Holiday was informed that she had cirrhosis of the liver. Her doctors told her she had to stop drinking, and for a short time,

Tombstone that marks the burial site of the great blues singer.

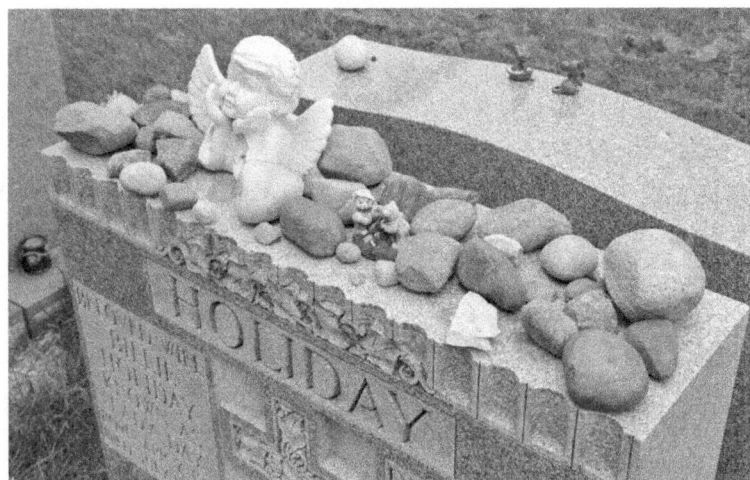

Grave goods left to honor Holiday show that she hasn't been forgotten.

she did. When she went back to the bottle, she hit it as hard as she ever had. On May 31, 1959, she was admitted to the Metropolitan Hospital in New York. While she was in her hospital bed, the police raided her room where she was arrested for possession of heroin, which was found in her purse. While she lay dying, a police guard was placed at her door.

She died from heart failure caused by cirrhosis on July 17, 1959. She was 44.

A few days later, her funeral was held at Saint Paul the Apostle Roman Catholic Church. More than 3,000 people attended it. She was laid to rest in Saint Raymond's Cemetery in the Bronx.

In 1972, Diana Ross starred as Holiday in the film *Lady Sings the Blues,* which was loosely based on the 1956 autobiography. The movie was a box office smash and was nominated for five Academy Awards. The city of Baltimore erected a statue in Holiday's honor that was dedicated in 1985. In 1988, U2 released the song "Angel of Harlem" as a tribute to Holiday.

One year before Holiday died, Frank Sinatra said, "It is Billie Holiday, whom I first heard on 52nd Street . . . who was and still remains the greatest single musical influence on me. It has been a warm and wonderful influence, and I am very proud to acknowledge it. Lady Day is unquestionably the most important influence on American popular singing in the last 20 years. With few exceptions, every major pop singer in the U.S. during her generation has been touched in some way by her genius."

If You Go:

The great boxing champion Hector (Macho) Camacho, who is regarded as one of the top fighters of his era, is buried here.

Singer Frankie Lymon of Frankie Lymon and the Teenagers was laid to rest here in 1968. When Lymon was only 13 years old, the group hit it big with the song "Why Do Fools Fall in Love."

Two-time typhoid epidemic source Mary "Typhoid Mary" Mallon can be found at Saint Raymond's, as can the actress Lois Nettleton who passed away in 2008.

14

Florence Foster Jenkins

"The Glory (????) of the Human Voice"

County: Luzerne • Town: Wilkes-Barre
Buried at Hollenback Cemetery
504 North River Street

Many said she had an unforgettable voice. One reporter described it as coming around but once in a generation, though he followed that observation by saying that was the public's good fortune. She was born into a wealthy Pennsylvania family and was well educated in the arts. She had a talent for the piano, but after an arm injury limited her options with that instrument, she decided she wanted to sing opera. The problem was her talent in this area was notably lacking. In his book documenting the world's heroic failures, Stephen Pile called her "the world's worst opera singer" writing that, "no one, before or since, has succeeded in liberating themselves quite so completely from the shackles of musical notation." This is not to say she has not had her admirers. In 1968 she was one of two singers mentioned by Barbara Streisand, who was responding to a query asking which other singers she would like to be. The other singer mentioned by Streisand was Ray Charles. In 2003 David Bowie cited the RCA album of her recordings as one of his most significant discoveries. She lived most of her adult life in New York City, and her crowning achievement came in 1944 when she performed in that city's Carnegie Hall. Lacking rhythm and pitch did not stand in the way of her becoming one of America's most famous sopranos. Her name was Florence Foster Jenkins.

Jenkins was born on July 19, 1868, in Wilkes-Barre, Pennsylvania. Her mother was Mary Jane Hoagland Foster, and her father, Charles Dorrance Foster, was a successful attorney and a descendant of wealthy

Florence Foster Jenkins

Pennsylvania landowners. The couple had only one other child, another daughter named Lillian, who contracted diphtheria and passed away at the age of eight in 1883.

As a girl, Jenkins developed a fondness for the piano, and her parents supported her interest in the instrument. She would later claim to have begun performing as a soloist at the age of ten, though other reports have her performing at society functions as "Little Miss Foster" when she was just seven years old. It is also possible that she performed for President

Rutherford B. Hayes when he visited Wilkes-Barre on July 3, 1878, where he was the principal speaker at the centennial commemoration of the Battle of Wyoming. In 2016 local Wilkes Barre historian, Anthony Brooks, said it was "absolutely plausible" that Jenkins met the president because her father served on the board of the Wyoming Commemorative Association.

At the age of ten, Jenkins was enrolled in a boarding school, the Moravian Seminary, located in Bethlehem, Pennsylvania. Though most of the students were Pennsylvania natives, those enrolled at Moravian included young women from all parts of the United States, as well as from Canada, England, and South American countries. The course of study leaned heavily on religion, and according to two of Jenkins biographers, Nicholas Martin and Jasper Rees, the goal of the institution was to produce "young women with an instinct for good behavior." Moravian did offer plenty of opportunities for her to continue with the piano as there were 46 of them on campus.

No one is certain when she met her husband, Dr. Frank Thornton Jenkins. He did have a sister, who also attended Moravian, so it is possible that their paths crossed when he was visiting. What we do know is that on June 29, 1883, Lillian Foster died, and ten days after the burial of her sister, the then 14-year old Jenkins eloped and married a man sixteen years her senior. The couple settled in Philadelphia. She left her husband after a year upon learning that he had infected her with syphilis. She would later claim to have been granted a divorce in 1902, but no documentation supporting this has ever been found. Though she never spoke to Dr. Jenkins again, she retained the surname for the rest of her life.

In 1886 Jenkins enrolled in a two-year course at the Philadelphia Academy of Music. Based on a report that appeared in an 1888 edition of the *Wilkes-Barre Record,* she appears to have done well at the academy. The paper reported that she was currently ranked second in a class of over 800. It described her as "a brilliant musician and is so considered in classical circles." After an arm injury ended any hopes Jenkins had of being a concert pianist, she gave piano lessons to support herself.

In 1909 her father died, and his will made Jenkins the beneficiary of a sizable trust. She and her mother moved to New York City, where she decided to pursue a musical career as a singer. She began taking singing lessons and joined multiple social clubs whose members were other wealthy New Yorkers. She began producing *tableaux vivants,* which were popular among the well-off in society at the time. Jenkins designed her elaborate costumes for her appearances at these events.

That first year in New York also brought another man into her life. Jenkins was forty years of age when she met a thirty-three-year-old English actor named St. Clair Bayfield. Years later, she recalled seeing Bayfield for the first time. "Why there is a man with the loveliest smile which I have ever seen in my life." She and Bayfield began a common-law relationship that would last the rest of her life.

Jenkins started singing at small musical events for her friends. She also performed on an annual basis in some larger venues like the Ritz Carlton ballroom. For these appearances, she refused to sell tickets to news reporters or critics, preferring an audience that consisted of friends and admirers. She soon became a musical cult figure in New York City, beginning in the roaring twenties and lasting until her death in 1944. She counted Cole Porter and Lily Pons among her fans. Porter rarely missed one of her recitals, but it was reported that he would bang his cane into his foot so he would not break out laughing when she sang. The poet Walter Meredith described her recitals as "never exactly an aesthetic experience, or only to the degree that an early Christian among the lions provided an aesthetic experience; it was chiefly immolatory, and Madame Jenkins was always eaten, in the end." The opera impresario Ira Siff said, "Jenkins was exquisitely bad, so bad that it added up to quite a good evening of theater."

In the early forties, Jenkins entered the Melotone Recording Studio in New York and, at her own expense, recorded nine selections on five 78 RPM records. She sold these to friends for $2.50. In the recordings, she was joined by her pianist, Cosme McMoon, who can be heard adjusting to her rhythm errors and consistent tempo variations. Still, there was little he could do about her delivering the numbers in a consistently flat manner. Seven of the selections were released by RCA Victor in 1954 and again in 1962 on a twelve-inch LP titled *The Glory (????) of the Human Voice.* This is the record David Bowie listed as one of his great discoveries. Sony Classical released a compact disc version in 1992.

At the age of 76, on October 25, 1944, prodded by public demand, Jenkins performed before a general admission audience at Carnegie Hall. A recreation of this concert was later featured in the movie *Florence Foster Jenkins* starring Meryl Streep in the title role. The film premiered in London and New York City in 2016. Streep received critical acclaim for her performance and an Academy Award nomination.

Tickets to the 2,800-seat venue sold out weeks in advance, and as many as 2,000 people were turned away at the door on the evening of the recital. Those who were able to gain entrance included Cole Porter (who certainly brought his cane); the renowned soprano Lily Pons (who was escorted by her husband the orchestra conductor, Andre Kostelanetz; burlesque star Gypsy Rose Lee; Kitty Carlisle; and the dance model for several Disney characters including Snow White, Marge Champion. Because Jenkins had no control over the sale of tickets, the audience also included multiple music critics and reporters.

When she appeared on the stage, she was greeted with a tremendous ovation that went on for several minutes. What followed was, in all probability, one of the most unusual shows in the hallowed hall's history. Marge Champion recalled, "I was just totally unprepared for the fact that it did not seem to bother her in the least that everyone in the audience was convulsed in laughter nor was she in any other way thrilled by it. I don't know what she did with it. I don't know how she processed that laughter."

A critic commented, "Her notes range from the impossible to the fantastic and bear no relationship whatsoever to any known score or scale."

McMoon sitting at his piano, remembered it as the noisiest audience he had ever performed before. When she delivered the song "Clavelitos," during which she tossed rosebuds at the audience, McMoon reported that one well-known actress was carried out of her box in a state of hysteria.

When he was leaving the concert, Earl Wilson of the *New York Post* ran into her common-law husband and asked, "Why?"

Bayfield replied, "She loves music."

Wilson responded, "If she loves music, why does she do this?"

The critics were not kind. Richard S. Davis wrote, "Mme. Jenkins, if you haven't heard, and the chances are you haven't, is a lady who gives

The grave of Florence Foster Jenkins

song recitals because there is no law against it. Mme. Jenkins bills herself as a coloratura soprano, which means that she takes the songs that bring out the best in Lily Pons and permits them to bring out her worst. And the worst of Mme. Jenkins, you are herewith assured, is something awful."

Whether she was bothered by the negative press, we will never know. She knew she had her detractors as years before Carnegie Hall she remarked to a friend, "People may say I can't sing, but no one can ever say I didn't sing."

Five days after the concert, Jenkins was shopping when she suffered a heart attack. She died one month later, on November 26, 1944, in her Manhattan residence. Her remains were returned to the city of her birth, and she was laid to rest in the Foster family mausoleum in Wilkes-Barre's Hollenback Cemetery.

15

Andy Kaufman

"Man on the Moon"

County: Nassau • Town: Elmont
Buried at Beth David Cemetery
300 Elmont Road

He began his comedic career working at numerous comedy clubs in the 1970s. He came to the national audience's attention when he made a critically acclaimed debut on *Saturday Night Live*. A character he called Foreign Man formed the basis for his role as Latka Gravas on the hit television show *Taxi*. When he played Carnegie Hall, he took the entire audience out for milk and cookies. His unique performances and elaborate comic ruses were so effective that many believed he had faked his death. Carl Reiner said of him, "Nobody can see past the edges, where the character begins, and he ends." Though hailed by some as a comic genius, he rejected the label saying, "I'm not trying to be funny, I just want to play with their heads." His name was Andy Kaufman. T'ank you veddy much.

Kaufman was born on January 17, 1949, in New York City. He was the first of Janice and Stanley Kaufman's three children. The family settled in a middle-class neighborhood located in Great Neck, Long Island. At a young age, Kaufman's childhood imagination, inspired by the early days of television, took over. The young boy would perform in his room before imaginary cameras. His shows aired daily, viewed by what he was sure had to be millions of people eager to see what he had up his sleeve on any given day. The shows involved singing and dancing and required the star to play multiple parts since Kaufman made up the entire cast and crew. Finally, his father grew worried about his oldest son spending so

Andy Kaufman, the man some would call a comic genius.

much time working on this imaginary show. He told Kaufman that performing was done before an audience and forbidding him from putting on his show without one. Determined not to disappoint his audience, he would lead his younger sister Carol to his room every day. She became his audience, and the show could go on.

Starting school cut into Kaufman's programming time. It was not possible to stage a show during school hours, so he was forced to seek out a secluded space during recess where he could entertain what he was sure was a legion of fans. Once, a classmate happened upon him as he was doing his show, and he stayed and watched for a short while. When he told others about Kaufman's antics, they came to see the show. He did not care that they thought he was crazy; they were just his live audience.

Kaufman began working children's birthday parties. These were his first gigs as a paid entertainer, and he used the techniques he had developed in his bedroom shows to great effect. He had a movie projector, and, in between his skits, he would show some of his favorite cartoons, including *Mighty Mouse*.

When Kaufman was a fourth-grader at the Baker Hill Elementary School, the Nigerian percussionist, Babatunde Olatunji, appeared at an assembly. A friend recalled that Kaufman was mesmerized by the show put on by the tall black man dressed in a dashiki, as he pounded and chanted, and he beat out his music to grades one through six. Kaufman left the assembly convinced that he would one day meet Olatunji and become his student. He did just that.

There were other influences. His grandfather introduced him to Elvis Presley, and it began a life-long love affair. Though few could rival Elvis, another teen idol captured Kaufman's attention. The young teenage boy named Fabian Forte, who had been discovered on his Philadelphia doorstep, was one of the young boy's favorites, especially a song that appeared on the B side of a 45 titled "This Friendly World." The song, much like the sound of the African drums, would always be important to him and to what others would later call his comic genius.

After Kaufman, to his parents' relief, graduated from high school, he enrolled at the Grahm Junior College in Boston. He decided to study television production in a two-year program offered by the institution. He made the dean's list, though one of the school's instructors would later recall that "he (Kaufman) really only blossomed in the performance courses" and that "he was always better when it was about him." He knocked the class and instructor out when each student performed the song "MacArthur Park" with a dramatic reading. Kaufman chose to read the song as an eighty-something-year-old Jewish man using a Yiddish dialect. "Someone left the cake out in the rain, Oyyy, I don't think that I can take it . . ." If he did not bring the house down, he did the classroom.

At Grahm, he produced and starred in his campus television show, *Uncle Andy's Fun House*. It was a children's show, and he used the talents that had served him so well in his bedroom and at birthday parties. He also began performing and working at local coffee houses. It was around this time; he began to develop the character known as Foreign Man.

Shortly after his first year in Boston, after he returned home for the summer, his high school girlfriend informed him that she was carrying his child. The baby arrived on July 19, 1969, and was put up for adoption. Kaufman would never set eyes on, let alone meet, his daughter.

After graduating from Grahm, he began doing stand-up comedy at clubs along the East Coast. By now, Foreign Man had evolved into a timid character, spoke in a high-pitched squeal with an accent, of course, who hailed from the fictional island of Caspiar, located somewhere in the Caspian Sea. By 1971, when he brought Foreign Man to the famed comedy club, The Improv, in New York City, Kaufman had the character down. It was a performance designed to make the audience uncomfortable because the performer was bombing so badly—so badly, in fact, that, by the time the people watching the show realized it was part of the act, their laughter had already made them a part of it. Foreign man would be introduced, and Kaufman would begin borrowing lines from other comics, but never getting to a punch line. "Tenk you veddy much. I am veddy happy to be here tonight, er, today, but you know there is vun thing I don't like about these places ees too much traffic. I had to come today on de highway, there was so much traffic eet took me an hour and a half to get here. But talk about terrible things, my wife, take my wife please take her . . ." The impersonation of the president of the United States would follow with Foreign Man never changing his high-pitched accented voice, "I am de president of the United States, make no mistake about that. Tank you veddy much!" Then Kaufman would announce that he was going to do Elvis Presley. He would turn his back to the audience, slick back his hair, give his head half a turn, and display the Presley sneer before delivering a hip-shaking rendition of a song Elvis had made famous with a voice resembling that of the great rock and roll star. Then, Foreign Man would return, take less than half a bow to the audience's continued applause and say, "Tank you veddy much."

On the stage, he was discovered by a young sports producer whom NBC had chosen to create a new comedy show that would air on Saturday nights in place of reruns of *The Tonight Show*. Given this project, Dick Ebersol began visiting New York clubs, searching for young talent. It was at Catch a Rising Star that he saw Kaufman for the first time. Ebersol soon became Kaufman's friend and a lifelong fan.

Ebersol recruited Lorne Michaels to join him in building the new show. Ebersol told Michaels that he already had one guest booked for the first show, Andy Kaufmann. Michaels had no idea who that was, so he, too, arranged to catch the young comic in action. As described in the Bill Zehme biography *Lost in the Funhouse*, Michaels was more than impressed. He later recalled, "It was as beautiful a thing as you could witness. Aside from being funny, he was not enmeshed in the show business of it— show business being that it was simply an act. There seemed to be some other commitment, something very pure and more personal about what he was doing. And it was simply arresting."

On October 11, 1975, *Saturday Night Live* made its debut. Kaufman, a firm believer and practitioner of

Kaufman shows his Latka face.

transcendental meditation locked himself in an office after posting a note on the door asking that he not be disturbed during meditation. Unknown to him, last-minute cuts were being made to the show to make sure it would fit into its ninety-minute time slot. Michael's insisted that Kaufman's spot not be cut. He took the stage in the show's first half-hour and stood next to a small record player. After placing the needle on a record, he stood by as the theme to the cartoon show *Mighty Mouse* began. He stood still, seemingly not part of the show, until the line "Here I come to save the day" came from the turntable, as Kaufman lip-synced the words with great enthusiasm. The studio audience, and those watching at home, lost it in laughter. Kaufman's short appearance became the talk of the show. He had nailed it, and, at the same time, forever doomed the act that had been part of his club show. He knew that using his Mighty Mouse on TV meant that he had to bury it as far as his future stage shows were concerned. After all, now everybody had already seen it. Tank you veddy much.

Kaufman was back on *Saturday Night Live* for the third and fourth shows. On November 3, Candice Bergen (who had caught his club act and was a big fan) introduced him by saying, "Boys and girls, this is a man I love very much. The word genius comes to mind, but I'll let you decide for yourself." This time, he did Foreign Man imitating Archie Bunker, ending with "de dingbat get into de kitchen making de food, ehh everybody is so stupid, tank you veddy much." As he continued his purposeful bomb, he forgot who he would imitate next, looking very uncomfortable, before offering to dance and sing. Now looking completely lost, and on live television, he looked to his side and asked, "ehh, could we stop de tape?" Then, he offered to turn off the TV as a solution before breaking down weeping, leading to yelping breaths that soon turned into perfect rhythms, as he accompanied himself on the conga. The new show had made him a new star in just a month.

The first big star to emerge from the regular *Saturday Night Live* cast was Chevy Chase. As recounted in Zehme's biography, Chase remembered conversations he had with Kaufman. "What's interesting is, behind those doors closed, we actually chuckled a lot. We had real laughs. Then, he would step out of the office and become the quiet, wide-eyed guy again. But those eyes were like the eyes of a tiger. They were always looking around for fresh prey."

In 1978, Foreign Man finally received a name. On September 12, the sitcom *Taxi* premiered on ABC. The show centered on a group of employees who worked for the fictional Sunshine Cab Company in Manhattan. The company's mechanic was an immigrant who, when excited, would revert to speaking in his native language (gibberish Kaufmann created), or when calm, in Foreign Man's accented voice. Kaufman resisted joining the cast, as he disliked sitcoms and certainly did not want to appear as a recurring character in one. Only the persistent prodding of his manager, George Shapiro, convinced the reluctant Kaufman to accept the role.

Kaufman approached the show in very much his own way. He was often late for rehearsals when he bothered to show up at all. He would leave the set and go off on his own to meditate. The rest of the cast, all professionals, began to take offense. Tony Danza, who played a slow-witted boxer forced to drive a cab to support himself, recalled, 'I always liked to say that he wouldn't have lasted long in my neighborhood." Once, when Kaufman made his usual late entrance, Danza took a fire extinguisher and sprayed the tardy cast member. Kaufman just stood there as Danza fired until the extinguisher was empty. He never reacted, and that only increased Danza's anger, who got his only reaction from the show's creator, James Brooks, who pulled Danza aside and told him, "Hey Tony, no soaking the actors."

With others writing the show and his lines, Kaufman grew weary of playing Latka. In response, the writers gave Latka multiple personality disorder, which allowed him to play other characters. One of these was the smooth-talking God's gift to women, Vic Ferrari. *TV Guide* named the episode titled "Latka the Playboy" number 19 of the top 100 greatest episodes of all time. Kaufman won two Golden Globe awards for his work on *Taxi*. Still, when the show was dropped after five seasons, Kaufmann saw it as a reason to celebrate.

Another of Kaufman's characters was Tony Clifton, a rude lounge singer, who made abusing his audience a habit. Kaufman claimed that Clifton was a real lounge singer he had once seen perform in Las Vegas when he went to see Elvis Presley in 1969. For a time, some believed that Clifton was a real performer. Promoters, who knew better, began booking Clifton to get Kaufman on the cheap. Kaufman would strike back using his friend Bob Zmuda to play the Clifton role while he made surprise appearances during the singer's act. Kaufman also used Clifton as his opening act for his stage shows. He would go on local news programs as Clifton to publicize the shows, and when Kaufman's name came up, he would get angry and complain that Kaufman was using him and his talent to get rich and famous.

Whether Kaufman used Clifton, in what may have been an effort to avoid having to take on the role of Latka, is up for debate. One of his demands, which Kaufman said was a deal-breaker, insofar as him taking the part on *Taxi*, was that Clifton be hired to appear on at least two episodes. The producers, perhaps to Kaufman's surprise, agreed.

The writers cast Clifton as Louie De Palma's (the head dispatcher at Sunshine Cab played by Danny DeVito) card-sharp brother Nicky, who hailed from Las Vegas. Clifton had his own demands when it came to appearing on the show. He refused to use Kaufman's dressing room, so a Winnebago trailer was provided. The vehicle came with a fully stocked bar. Also, two tall blond women were hired to accompany Clifton during the filming. Clifton and his entourage arrived on the set in a pink

Kaufman impersonates a president.

Cadillac. Unlike Kaufman, Clifton was on the set early and made a point of complaining about everyone who arrived after him. He also carried a smell with him, a combination of whiskey, cigarettes, and the body odor of a person who loathed bathing. With a bottle of Jack Daniels in hand, he hit on every woman who showed themselves and cast member Marilu Henner. His script readings were beyond awful, and it became evident that there was no way they could put an episode together that included Clifton. Kaufman was contacted and told that Clifton had to be fired. Rather than fight it, Kaufman said he understood, but asked that the firing be blamed not on his acting ability, but on his drinking, or his arrival late, which he said would be arranged for the next day. The relieved producers agreed. The next day Clifton put up a tremendous fight, and security had to be called to remove him from the set as he yelled at all present, "I will be back one day when I play Vegas. None of you will get in when I play. I'll be a big star." Tony Clifton was banned from ever setting foot on the set, at any time, ever again.

To prepare for a show at Carnegie Hall that would fulfill a lifelong dream, Kaufman performed what might be called a rehearsal, in front of a live audience, at the Huntington Hartford Theater in Hollywood. Clifton opened the show for Kaufman, who finally bounded onto the stage, himself, to the tune "Oklahoma." He promised the audience special treats later if they behaved themselves. He wrestled a woman from the audience, who he pinned, only to have a large man bound on the stage calling Kaufman a "skinny geek" and challenging him to take on a man. The intruder was a trained Hollywood stunt man, who began to toss Kaufmann all around the stage expertly. In the audience, Kaufman's mother, who was with her husband and her son's *Taxi* co-star, Judd Hirsch, began to panic. She was screaming for someone to help her son, and as Hirsch remembers, she grabbed him by the wrists, yelling, "Oh my God, He's gonna get killed." Hirsch had just met Kaufman's parents and now began to wonder if he had been placed next to someone in the act who was playing a family member. Then Zmuda, dressed as a referee, came to the rescue, rushing to Kaufman with a can of spinach, which Kaufman pretended to consume. Soon, he was on his feet, tossing the stuntman around the stage to the tune of "Popeye the Sailor Man." Foreign Man made an appearance, and Andy led the audience in a singalong of "This Friendly World." Later, he introduced the Rockettes and the Mormon Tabernacle Choir, though it was clear to the audience that the ladies were not Rockettes, and the all-black gospel singers had not made the trip from Salt Lake City. Then, he gave the audience their treat, informing them that buses were out front waiting, and he was taking them all for milk and cookies. That is just what he did.

Later, he would perform much the same show at Carnegie Hall. One difference was a very comfortable chair was set on the stage for an old woman that Kaufman identified as his grandmother. He explained he wanted her to have a good seat for this show since it was the culmination of a dream they shared. Later in the show, it was revealed that the woman watching the show from the stage was Robin Williams. Another difference in the show was that, in New York, it took 24 buses to take the audience for milk and cookies, in contrast to the ten that had been used in Hollywood.

Wrestling women, as he did at Carnegie Hall, became part of Kaufman's stage act. He called himself the Inter-Gender Wrestling Champion of the World. He eventually played the wrestling angle into a public feud with the very real Memphis professional wrestler Jerry "The King" Lawler. Before stepping into the ring with Lawler in his hometown, Kaufman taunted the residents of Memphis. He filmed slow-motion videos to teach the locals how to use soap, and he referred to Memphis as "the nation's redneck capital."

Kaufman and Lawler agreed to meet in the ring. The two choreographed their bout a couple of days before the event, set for April 5, 1982. Twelve thousand people booed as Kaufman entered the ring. He let Lawler chase him around the ring for about five minutes, jumping outside the ropes whenever the wrestler got close. Finally, Lawler motioned to Kaufman that he could put him in a headlock to start. Kaufman's hold did not last long. In a matter of seconds, Lawler picked him up and threw him onto the canvas. Picking Kaufman up, Lawler then used an illegal hold—a pile-driver—to slam Kaufman's head onto the ring's floor. He repeated this twice. Though they had practiced the move, Kaufman was not a professional wrestler, and the force of the blows injured him, jamming his neck. With Kaufman prone on the canvas, an ambulance was summoned while the crowd roared its delight.

Wearing a neck brace that he donned whenever he appeared in public for the next five months, Kaufmann announced his retirement from wrestling. He then went back to the *Letterman* show, where he offered Lawler forgiveness and wished for an apology. In late July, the two combatants were reunited on *Letterman*. The plan was for the two to watch the match and give the appearance of remaining enemies. After a commercial, the two would apologize, and Kaufman would sing "What the World Needs Now (Is Love, Sweet Love)." With the agreement in place, Lawler headed to his hotel, where he received Kaufman's call. During their conversation, Kaufman said that he wondered what would happen if Lawler hit him instead of apologizing. Lawler recalled that he did not ask me to do it, but he made it clear that he wanted it to happen.

When they appeared on the show and watched the footage, Kaufman said he was trying to have some fun. Lawler said he was uncomfortable sitting next to a wimp. After the commercial, Kaufman said he had made a mistake in wrestling Lawler and felt he was owed an apology. Lawler disagreed and said he did not know if Kaufman was wearing a neck brace or a flea collar. The response surprised Letterman, who was waiting for the apology. Instead, Kaufman grew agitated and started saying he was going to sue Lawler. Letterman tried to go to another commercial, but before he could do it, Lawler stood up and slapped Kaufman, knocking him to the floor. They had to stop taping the show as Kaufman began screaming that he wanted Lawler arrested.

When the show finally resumed, Kaufman took it even further. First, he refused to return to the stage, then, as described by Zehne, he burst back on the set and stood behind Letterman, yelling, "I'm sick of this bullshit! You are full of bullshit, my friend! I will sue you for everything you have! I will sue your ass! You're a motherfuckin' asshole, as far as I'm concerned! You hear me! A fuckin' asshole! Fuck you! I will get you for this!" Kaufman then started to walk away before taking an about-face to return and say, "I am sorry, I am sorry to use those words on television. I apologize to all my fans. I'm sorry, I'm sorry, but you—you're a fuckin' asshole!" Slamming his hand on Letterman's desk, he repeated, "You hear me! A fuckin' asshole!" He then grabbed Letterman's coffee cup and sent its contents in Lawler's direction. In response, the wrestler rose from his seat, sending Kaufman running from the stage. Letterman turned to the audience and said, "Uhh, I think you can use some of those words on TV . . . but what you can't do is throw coffee." During the break, Kaufman had asked someone on the show if he was taking it too far. He was told, no, that it was great entertainment.

In 1983, over Thanksgiving, family members told Kaufman that they were worried about his persistent coughing. Upon his return to Los Angeles, he went through a series of medical tests. He was diagnosed with an extremely rare case of lung cancer. He died on May 16, 1984, at the age of 35. He was laid to rest in the family plot located in Beth David Cemetery in Elmont, New York.

In 1992, the band R.E.M. released the song "Man on the Moon," a tribute to Kaufman, and the song's video included film footage of the late comedian. In 1995, NBC aired *A Comedy Salute to Andy Kaufmann*. In

Here lies the man on the moon.

1999, Jim Carrey portrayed Kaufman in the film *Man on the Moon*. In Los Angeles, at The Comedy Store, a neon likeness of Kaufman can be found. You can also order the Andy Kaufman Special, and, if you do, you will get two cookies and a glass of milk.

If You Go:
Dr. Eduard Bloch, the personal physician to Adolf Hitler's family, is buried at Beth David. Bloch treated Hitler for a serious lung ailment in 1904. He also treated Hitler's mother, never charging the family when she was dying of breast cancer. Hitler protected the Jewish doctor from the Gestapo, and Bloch and his family left Germany in 1940. Psychologist and television personality Dr. Joyce Brothers was laid to rest here, as was the noted composer Bernard Herrmann, who is best remembered for his films. Herrmann began his work in movies with *Citizen Kane* and finished with *Taxi Driver*. He won an Academy Award for his work on *The Devil and Daniel Webster*. The actor best known for his work in the movie *The Godfather* and on television for his role as Sgt. Phil Fish in the sitcom *Barney Miller*, Abe Vigoda, can also be found at Beth David.

16

Dorothy Kilgallen

"What's My Line?"

County: Westchester • Town: Hawthorne
Buried at Gate of Heaven Cemetery
10 West Stevens Road

She grew up admiring her father, who was an accomplished journalist for the Hearst corporation newspapers. Following in his footsteps, she began her career as a reporter for the *New York Evening Journal*. She rose to fame, competing in an around the world race with two rival newspapermen. She then did a short stint in Hollywood, writing a column that shared news and gossip about the nation's movie stars. A successful radio career followed. In the 1950s, she was one of the original celebrity panelists on the popular TV show *What's My Line*. Simultaneously, her syndicated column, *The Voice of Broadway*, was enormously popular throughout the country. In the mid-1960s, she was working on a book that she informed friends would blow the lid off the Warren Commission's report on President John F. Kennedy's assassination. Her mysterious death raises questions to this very day. Her name was Dorothy Kilgallen.

Kilgallen was born on July 3, 1913, in Chicago. By 1920, after a series of moves, the family settled in Brooklyn. Her father, James Kilgallen, was a newspaper reporter and was often away from home, searching out stories for his employer, the Hearst Corporation. Though she attended a public school, Kilgallen was raised Catholic. While her grades were good in both elementary and high school, she failed to make a distinct impression on either her classmates or teachers. By 1930, the young woman was attending the College of New Rochelle, an institution whose purpose was to educate Catholic women. In the summer of 1931, she accepted

Dorothy Kilgallen

a summer job working for the New York Journal. When she was leaving school to head to work that summer, one of the nuns, who had advised her to accept the position, told Kilgallen, "Be sure to come back in the fall." Neither the nun nor Kilgallen knew her school days were over.

Kilgallen had always wanted to follow her father into the newspaper business, and this summer job gave her that chance. Her first boss was the paper's assistant city editor, Garry Finley, who had been told to go easy on Jim Kilgallen's girl. The problem was that Finley was not particularly fond of newspaper women, and he did not care who Kilgallen's father was. In an early discussion, Kilgallen told Finley that she had never seen a dead body and avoided looking at the deceased when she attended a wake. With that information in hand, he assigned his new cub reporter to the morgue, where her job would be to describe suicide victims in a manner that would aid friends and relatives to identify the victims. While working this beat, she found that chewing gum helped get her through the experience.

Kilgallen as a CBS reporter.

It turned out to be a habit not easily broken. According to Kilgallen's biographer, Lee Israel, in 1936, another Hearst reporter wrote a piece describing Kilgallen, covering a murder science. The story read, "It was an extremely messy murder, which left indiscreet scraps of evidence littering a vacant lot . . . Yet there, amid the messiness, stood the epitome of all Innocent Young Girls . . . little Miss Kilgallen, meek, mum Minnie Mousish, chewing the world's record wad of gum, and coolly making corking copy of each bloody thread."

That same year, Kilgallen took part in a race around the world that brought her to the entire nation's attention. The race was inspired by a similar trip made by a 23-year-old woman reporter named Nellie Bly (see Chapter 4) in 1889. Bly was working for Joseph's Pulitzer's *New York World* when the paper sent her around the world to beat the fictional record set by the character Phineas Fogg in Jules Verne's *Around the World in 80 days.* Bly made the trip in 72 days. Speed was a national obsession in the 1930s, with faster automobiles, ocean liners, and airplanes taking center stage. Kilgallen's newspaper sent her on a race against two male rival reporters, with the object being to make the journey in 21 days. The first leg of the journey saw Kilgallen and her competitors make their way to Lakehurst, New Jersey, to board the German dirigible, *Hindenburg,* for the trans-Atlantic flight. The famous aviator, Amelia Earhart, was among those who stated their support for Kilgallen in the contest, even offering Kilgallen advice on maintaining her usual schedule of eating and sleeping on the trip. Kilgallen's daily dispatches, noting her progress, captured the attention of the whole country. At a regularly scheduled press conference held by President Franklin Delano Roosevelt's campaign manager James Farley (see *Gotham Graves Volume One*), the first question he fielded was "Where's Dorothy now?" Though Kilgallen failed to win the race, she had won nationwide recognition that would stay with her the rest of her life. Even the first lady, Eleanor Roosevelt, wrote her a letter congratulating her on her effort, noting that she was "rather pleased" that a woman had made a go of it.

Fresh off the trip, Kilgallen was dispatched to Hollywood and given the assignment of writing a column covering the nation's movie stars. She was just 23 years old when she began writing the column titled *Hollywood Scene as Seen by Dorothy Kilgallen*. While in Hollywood, she also appeared in a feature film, playing a reporter in the movie *Sinner take All*. Her five lines in the movie were cut to one, and the experience soured her on acting. Years later, she was asked whether she had once appeared in a movie, and she replied, "What on earth ever gave you that idea?"

Kilgallen preferred New York City to Hollywood, and, in 1938, she returned to the Big Apple, where she began writing another daily column titled *The Voice of Broadway*. This gossip column grew in popularity and eventually found its way into syndication, appearing in 146 newspapers. Kilgallen covered New York show business and celebrity gossip while, at times, touching on politics and organized crime stories. The still youthful newspaperwoman would author *The Voice* until the day she died.

As far as her personal life went, Kilgallen dated a few men during this period, including the movie star Tyrone Power, whom she had met during her time in Hollywood. She had also attended a musical comedy where an actor named Richard Kollmar made his Broadway debut. Soon, flattering mentions of Kollmar began appearing in her column. The actor's press agent called Kilgallen and arranged a luncheon date between the two. After a few more dates, he proposed, and the two were wed on

April 6, 1940. Those who attended the wedding included Jimmy Walker, James Farley, Eddy Duchin, Walter Huston, Milton Berle, and Ethel Merman. The couple raised three children, though the marriage had its share of rocky moments fueled by Kollmar's affairs and her relationship with the singer Johnnie Ray.

By 1941, Kilgallen appeared on a weekly radio show also called *The Voice of Broadway.* Her husband was also showcasing his singing talent on both the Broadway stage and on various radio shows. In 1945, the duo began co-hosting their radio show titled *Breakfast with Dorothy and Dick* from their Park Avenue apartment. The show, which also mixed gossip with serious issues, was an immediate hit and remained on the air long after the termination of other radio shows the two had worked on alone.

In 1950, the show *What's My Line* made its television debut. The show proved to be a smashing success, running until 1967, and Kilgallen was an original panelist. On February 2, the show premiered and was hosted by the newsman John Daly, who began the show by using his foot to stomp out a cigarette before introducing the first guest and asking them to "sign in, please." The initial contestant dutifully signed "Pat Finch" on a small blackboard before taking her seat next to Daly, facing Kilgallen and the other panelists. The studio audience and those watching at home were informed that Finch was a hat check girl. Kilgallen posed the first question, asking, "Are you engaged in selling services as opposed to a product?" Later in the program, a diaper executive faced the panel and responded to Kilgallen's question, "Would you consider this product a necessity?" Daly stepped in and answered with a modified "no." When the host revealed the man's profession, Kilgallen insisted that the panel had been misled. New York Yankee shortstop Phil Rizzuto was the mystery guest. Still, Kilgallen, who had donned the obligatory mask so she could not identify the well-known guest, complained, "If diapers aren't a necessity, I don't know what is." The show gained Kilgallen nationwide recognition.

Though *What's My Line* was intended to provide light entertainment and comedic moments, Kilgallen took it quite seriously. She was very competitive and would go into a funk and sulk when she failed to guess

Kilgallen lunching with Eddie Cantor, 1941.

a contestant's occupation or a mystery guest's identity. Fellow panelist Bennett Serf recalled that, unlike her peers, who were looking to entertain the audience, Kilgallen was mainly interested in winning. Cerf also said that she would extend her time on camera by asking questions that she knew would elicit a positive reply so that she would not lose her turn.

Though she was now both a radio and television star, Kilgallen continued to receive plum newspaper assignments. In 1953, she covered the coronation of Queen Elizabeth. Her work, which garnered front-page attention, resulted in a Pulitzer Prize nomination.

The following year, she was sent to Cleveland to cover the Doctor Sam Sheppard murder trial. Sheppard, whose story would inspire the television show *The Fugitive,* was on trial for the bludgeoning death of his wife. When Kilgallen arrived in the courtroom, she was informed that the judge would like to see her. She was then escorted to the chambers of Judge Edward Blythin, who expressed his pleasure at meeting the newspaperwoman and noted that he watched her often on television. When the judge asked her what about the case had brought her to Cleveland,

Kilgallen with Arthur Miller and Marilyn Monroe.

she told him that it had all the makings of what the newspaper business would call a "good murder," adding that there was also the mystery of who did it. The judge responded by telling her there was no mystery and that Sheppard was "guilty as hell."

When Sheppard was found guilty and sentenced to life in prison, Kilgallen was very critical of the verdict, so critical in fact, that a Cleveland newspaper dropped her column. More than nine years later, she told her story of her meeting with the judge before a crowd that included F. Lee Bailey, Sheppard's attorney. Bailey deposed Kilgallen and included that deposition in a petition to the courts on behalf of his client. Sheppard was released, retried, and acquitted.

In 1956, the 29-year-old singer, Johnnie Ray, appeared as the mystery guest on *What's My Line.* After that, Kilgallen and Ray began seeing each other regularly. Close friends say Kilgallen fell totally in love with Ray. It reached the point where the singer had to tell Kilgallen to go easy on the references to him in her column. When possible, she would also travel to see Ray perform when he was on the road. When Ray appeared in Chicago, she told him she wanted to go to another club to see a comic she heard about named Lenny Bruce. Ray knew both Bruce and his work, and he tried to talk Kilgallen out of it with no success. When the two arrived at the club, Ray went backstage and warned Bruce that Kilgallen was present and that it would be in the comic's best interests to keep the show clean. Bruce responded by saying, "Give me a kiss on the cheek and get out of here." Bruce opened his show with a discussion of oral copulation, and Ray was convinced he was witnessing the end of the comic's career. As the show went on, Kilgallen's giggles turned to laughs, and she became one of Bruce's prominent supporters.

In the mid-1950s, Kilgallen began including references to an old friend, Frank Sinatra, in her columns. Her stories referenced Sinatra's woes relative to his marriage with Ava Gardner. She wrote that, when Gardner left the singer, an agent was assigned to keep him from slashing his wrists. Kilgallen painted a picture of Sinatra that was anything but flattering, saying that success hadn't changed the man—he remained "hot-tempered, egotistical, extravagant, and moody." Sinatra struck back from the stage during performances when he would compare Kilgallen's face to a chipmunk's, and he began calling her the "chinless wonder." Kilgallen insisted that Sinatra's ire resulted from her spurning his sexual advances and had nothing to do with her columns.

By the early 1960s, drinking and barbiturate abuse began to affect her behavior. The producer of *What's My Line*, Mark Goodson, grew concerned when he began receiving letters from viewers noting her thick speech on camera. Goodson approached Kilgallen, urging her to seek help and suggesting that she see a psychiatrist. Kilgallen responded, "I don't need a psychiatrist. I'm a Catholic."

On November 22, 1963, like most Americans, Kilgallen was shocked when she learned of President John F. Kennedy's assassination. Following Kennedy's death, her column told the story of her taking her youngest son to meet Kennedy in the White House. On the day following the assassination, she and her son watched the coverage of the events on television in tears. The following February, Kilgallen headed to Dallas to attend Jack Ruby's trial, who had killed Kennedy's alleged assassin before a live television audience.

When she appeared in the courtroom, she was invited to join the judge in his chambers. The judge wisely refused to discuss the case, but it was clear that he was a Kilgallen fan. On this trip to Dallas, Kilgallen established a working relationship with Ruby's attorneys. Through them, she began to doubt the government's official position that Lee Harvey Oswald alone had killed the president with no help from others.

Kilgallen's columns began to reflect her doubt, and she wondered in print, "Who was Oswald, Anyway?" One day, during a court recess, Ruby's attorney informed her that Ruby wanted to talk with her. After this get together in the courtroom, she arranged for a private interview with Oswald's killer. The two were together for about eight minutes, and Kilgallen stored her interview notes in a file she had started on the assassination. She began working on a book and told friends that she would "blow the JFK case sky high."

On November 7, 1965, she arrived at the studio to film an episode of *What's My Line*. Kilgallen successfully deduced the occupation of two of the guests. After the show, she went to P. J. Clarke's with a friend for drinks. She informed her friend that she had a late date and left a bit after midnight. She was next seen sitting alone in the cocktail lounge of the Regency Hotel at around one o'clock. Sometime the next morning, Kilgallen was found dead, sitting up in her bed, a book by her side. Her father reported that she had died because of a heart attack.

Though her husband objected, Kilgallen's body was taken to the medical examiner's office for an autopsy. When the death certificate was issued, the cause was identified as "acute ethanol and barbiturate intoxication, circumstances undetermined." According to the report, Kilgallen had died because of too much liquor and drugs. It was not possible to determine whether the death was accidental. To most, this meant that Kilgallen had overdosed accidentally or had committed suicide. Over

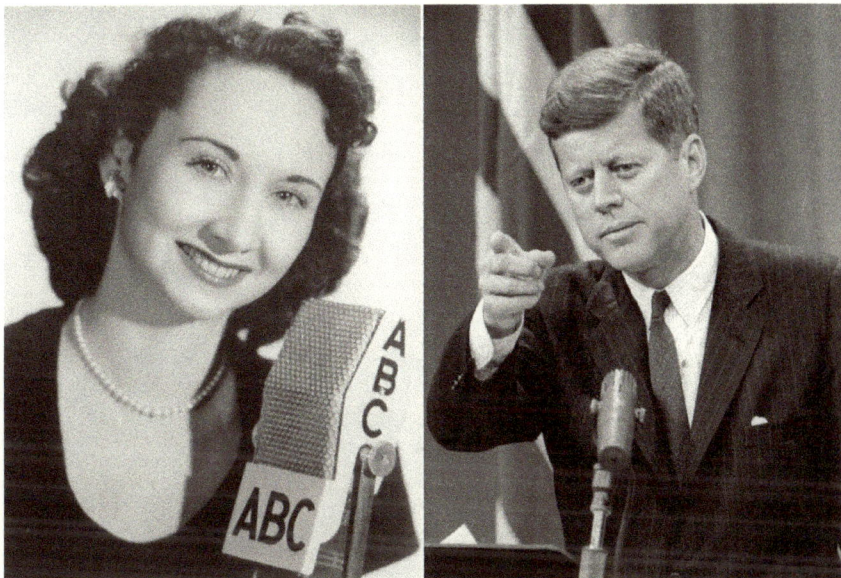

Kilgallen's death may have been linked to the JFK assassination.

time, others brought up another possibility when they asked, "Was Dorothy Kilgallen murdered?"

As detailed in the book *Hit List* by Richard Belzer and David Wayne, Kilgallen's death raised numerous questions. Her body was discovered in a bed where both her family and friends knew that she never slept. Her hairdresser, who is credited with discovering the body, told others, "When I tell you the bed she was found in, and how I found her, you're going to know she was murdered." When she was found, she was wearing a bolero type blouse over her nightgown; something friends say she would never wear to bed. She was still wearing makeup and false eyelashes when her body was discovered. The book that was found on her bed was one that she had told friends she had already read. She used reading glasses, yet none were found near her. Tests on a glass found near the bed showed one type of barbiturate, even though her autopsy concluded that her death resulted from a lethal combination of three barbiturates and alcohol. The air conditioning, which she never slept with on, was running. All these factors have led some to conclude that the death scene was staged.

Modest tombstone of the great female reporter.

A review of Kilgallen's death hardly supports that it was the result of suicide. She showed no signs of depression and was very excited about the information that would appear in her forthcoming book, as she had told friends. In the early morning hours on the day of her death, she had called Western Union to pick up her column for the next day's newspaper. Also, if she had wanted to kill herself, a far higher dosage of drugs would likely have been discovered during the autopsy. As it was, what was found was just enough to kill her.

Kilgallen's biographer, Lee Israel, wrote that, after spending three years investigating the events relating to Kilgallen's death, "it is clear to me that she did not die accidentally and that a network of varied activities, impelled by disparate purposes, conspired effectively to obfuscate the truth." In the last months of her life, Israel also notes that Kilgallen had befriended a man named Ron Pataky, who may have had links to U. S. Intelligence agencies. According to Israel, Pataky "enrolled in a training school for assassins in Panama or thereabouts." When asked directly whether Pataky had murdered Kilgallen, Israel responded, "he had something to do with it." Kilgallen's file on the JFK assassination, including her notes from her interview with Jack Ruby, have never been found.

After Kilgallen's death, Warren Commission critic Mark Lane responded to audiences, who laughed when he brought her name up during lectures, with a standard response. "You're laughing because you think of her as a gossip columnist. Well, I'm gonna tell you something. She was a very, very, serious journalist. You might say she was the only serious journalist in America who was concerned with who killed John Kennedy and getting all the facts about the assassination."

More than ten thousand mourners filed past Kilgallen's casket before her being laid to rest in the Gate of Heaven Cemetery.

If You Go:

There are several famous graves to be found at Gate of Heaven Cemetery. The great actor James Cagney (see *Gotham Graves Volume One*, Chapter 4) rests here. Yankee player and manager Billy Martin can be found not far from the grave of Franklin Delano Roosevelt's trusted campaign manager James Farley (see *Gotham Graves Volume One*, Chapter 6).

17

Nancy Kulp

"Slim"

County: Juniata • Town: Mifflintown
Buried at Westminster Presbyterian Cemetery
Mifflintown, Pennsylvania

Nancy Kulp was a character actress and comedienne best known for her role on the CBS television series *The Beverly Hillbillies*. She had a varied and interesting life as a journalist, actress, comedienne, publicity person, a decorated lieutenant in the US Naval Reserve, and a politician.

Nancy Jane Kulp was born in Harrisburg, Pennsylvania, as the only child of Robert Tilden Kulp and Marjorie Kulp on August 28, 1921. The family later moved to Dade County, Florida. Nancy was a studious child and dreamed of becoming a journalist. She took a major step toward that goal by graduating from Florida State University in 1943 with a bachelor's degree in journalism. She then went on for a master's degree in English and French at the University of Miami. During this time, she worked as a writer at the *Miami Beach Tropics* newspaper, writing many celebrity profiles, including ones on Clark Gable and Errol Flynn.

In 1944 she left the University of Miami to join the WAVES. She rose to the rank of Lieutenant and received several decorations. She was honorably discharged in 1946.

Returning to civilian life, she took a job as publicity director at a Miami radio station (WGBS) and a few years later moved to a television station where she directed and acted.

In 1951 Kulp married Charles Malcolm Dacus and then moved to Hollywood, California, to work in MGM's publicity department. The couple divorced ten years later in 1961, and Kulp refused to discuss him when asked.

Nancy Kulp

Her big break came shortly after she started at MGM when Director George Cukor convinced her to try acting and cast her in his film *The Model and the Marriage Broker*. This role was Kulp's first as the sort of character she would often play, the spinster. The movie was successful and led to roles in *Steel Town* and *The Marrying Kind* in 1952.

The next two years saw Kulp land roles in *Shane*, starring Alan Ladd; *Sabrina*, directed by Billy Wilder and starring Audrey Hepburn and Humphrey Bogart; and *A Star Is Born*, starring Judy Garland and again directed by George Cukor. During this time, she guest-starred in *Topper* and *December Bride* television shows. In 1955 she joined the cast as a regular character on *The Bob Cummings Show*, also known as *Love that Bob*. It was her first recurring TV role. She played a neighborhood bird watcher named Pamela Livingstone. Kulp actually was a bird watcher. The show ended in 1959.

From the time she appeared on the *Bob Cummings Show* until 1962, Kulp found a lot of work in movies and television. She was cast in comedies like *You're Never Too Young* (1955) with Martin and Lewis and *Forever Darling* with Lucille Ball and Desi Arnaz, and dramas like the Academy Award-winning *Three Faces of Eve* (1957), starring Joanne Woodward. *The Parent Trap* and *Strange Bedfellows* are among the many other movies she appeared.

Her television appearances during this period were numerous. She appeared on such hit shows as *Cheyenne*, *I Love Lucy*, *The Real McCoys*, *The Twilight Zone*, *Maverick*, *Mister Ed*, *The Jack Benny Show*, *77 Sunset Strip*, and multiple episodes of *Perry Mason* and *My Three Sons*. She also had recurring roles on *Our Miss Brooks* and *Date with The Angels*. These are just some of the many shows on which Kulp appeared.

Shortly after her performances on *My Three Sons* in 1962, Kulp landed her breakout role as the prim, efficient Miss Jane Hathaway, secretary to banker Milburn Drysdale. She and Drysdale were managing the millions of dollars of the Clampett family, a backwoods clan who had relocated from Tennessee to Beverly Hills after striking oil. The humor arose from the contrast between the Clampetts who made moonshine and kept "critters" and the up-scale Southern Californians. Buddy Ebsen played the role of Jed Clampett, head of the Clampett family. Though their characters were miles apart in personal philosophy and worldview, which was often the brunt of the jokes on screen, the disconnect between the two stars didn't stop when the cameras quit rolling. Kulp and Ebsen were reported to have a very combative relationship on set, often arguing over politics and personal disagreements. Ebsen, a lifelong conservative Republican, commonly quarreled with the more liberal Kulp. Both were former naval officers, and their disputes became a common occurrence. Over the years, numerous cast members have commented on their tumultuous relationship, claiming that calm discussions would regularly escalate to yelling and name-calling. Their contentious relationship continued well beyond the show's run.

Critics had no love for the show, but viewers kept it rated high. It ran for nine seasons and accumulated seven Emmy nominations, including one for Kulp in 1967 for Supporting Actress in a Comedy, and had extended life syndication.

After *The Beverly Hillbillies* ended in 1971, she continued to guest star on various TV series; she had a recurring role on *Sanford and Son* and appeared on *The Love Boat* and *Fantasy Island*. She also performed on Broadway in *Mornings at Seven* in 1980-81.

In 1984, Kulp, who had long been interested in politics, decided to run for congress in her district in central Pennsylvania, having settled in Port Royal. She ran as a Democrat against the ninth district's incumbent Republican, Bud Shuster. She ran a diligent campaign even though she was unlikely to win the seat that had been Republican for twelve years. Even with polls indicating she was almost sure to lose, Ebsen felt he needed to get his jab in. He recorded radio and television ads for Shuster, claiming she was too liberal for Pennsylvania. Kulp was enraged by Ebsen, a California resident getting involved. She stated she "was speechless at such a betrayal and something so needless and cruel." She did receive an endorsement from a friend and showbiz personality, Ed Asner. She lost the race and did not speak to Ebsen for several years afterward but eventually claimed to have made peace with him. The fact that he contacted the Shuster campaign and volunteered to make the ads really hurt and outraged her. In his later years, Ebsen privately expressed remorse for doing the ads and claimed they only reconciled shortly before Kulp's death.

After the election, Kulp accepted an artist-in-residence position teaching film and drama at Juniata College. She later returned to California to serve on the board of the Screen Actors Guild and took an active role in many non-profits

In 1989, Kulp came out as a lesbian in an interview with the author Boze Hadleigh. Her exact words read, "as long as you reproduce my reply word for word, and the question, you may use it . . . I'd appreciate it if

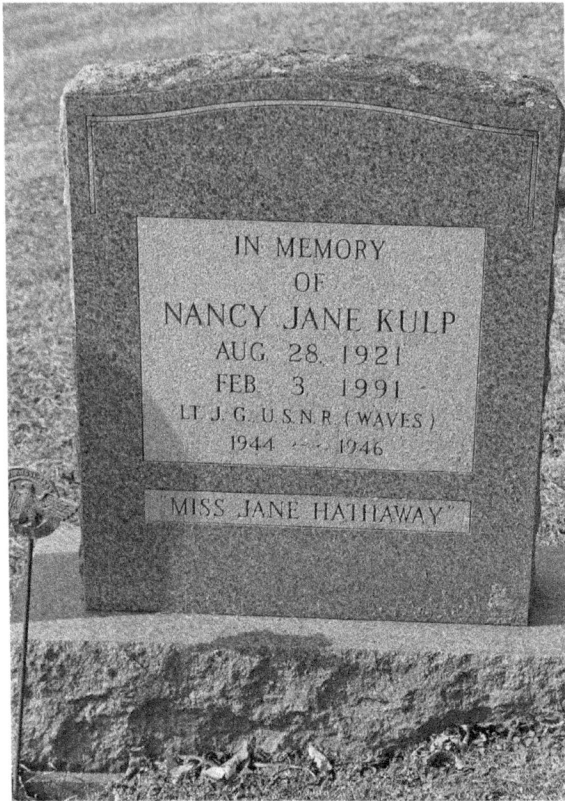

Kulp's grave

you'd let me phrase the question. There is more than one way. Here's how I would ask it: 'Do you think that opposites attract?' My own reply would be that I'm the other sort—I find that birds of a feather flock together. That answers your question."

Nancy Kulp was diagnosed with cancer in 1990 and underwent chemotherapy. However, it spread rapidly, and she died on February 3, 1991, at a friend's house in Palm Desert, California. She was 69 years old. She was buried at the Westminster Presbyterian Cemetery in Mifflintown, Pennsylvania.

18

John Lennon

"Give Peace a Chance"

County: Manhattan • Town: New York
Buried at Strawberry Fields Section of Central Park
Between 71st and 74th Streets

He was born while Hitler's Luftwaffe was pounding England during the Battle of Britain. His father left him when he was still a young child, and his mother's family sent him to her older sister to care for and raise him. At school, he developed a reputation as a troublemaker whose chances for future success were slim. He would go on to publish two critically acclaimed books, lead a band that would revolutionize music worldwide, come to be recognized as one of the greatest composers of his time, and earn the well-deserved title of a peace activist. If Bob Dylan was the "Voice of a Generation," then he was its conscience. A musician, a poet, a philosopher, and a humanitarian is how the world came to know John Lennon.

On October 9, 1940, John Lennon took center stage for the first time. As soon as she had been informed of his arrival, Lennon's Aunt Mimi ran to the hospital, ducking into doorways to dodge the bombs being dropped by the Germans. At the time of his birth, Lennon's father, Alfred, was fittingly at sea working as a ship steward. It proved fitting because his father's absence would be the norm in Lennon's life. His mother, Julia, was beautiful and free-spirited. She had married Alfred against her family's wishes.

Alfred Lennon returned to port after one of his sea trips to find Julia pregnant by another man. To the surprise of few, the marriage failed, but not before scarring the young Lennon. Alfred received permission from

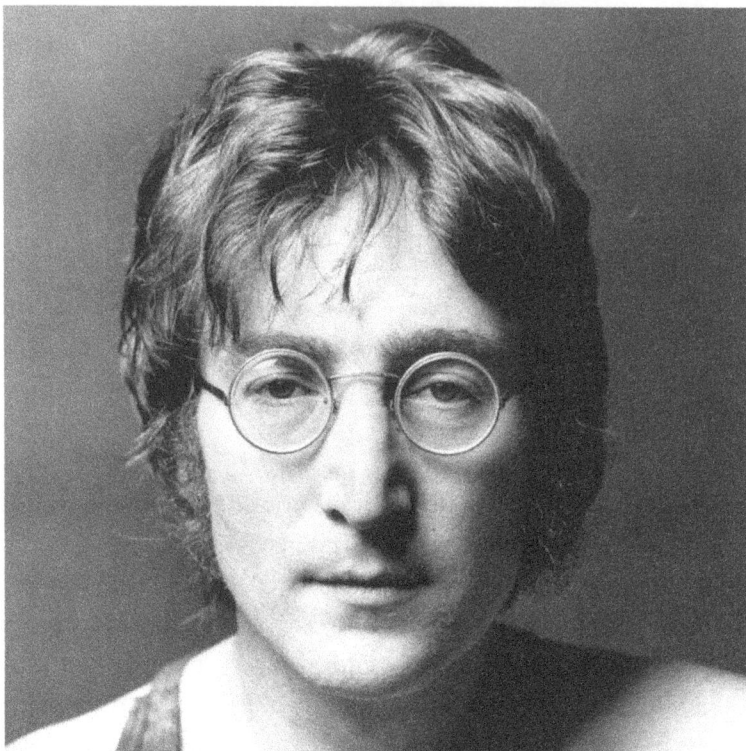

John Lennon

Julia to take his son on a day trip. Lennon's father's real plan was to have his brother adopt the boy. When the day trip turned into a multiple day trip, Julia did some detective work and tracked down Alfred and Lennon. It was Alfred who presented the four-year-old with a Hobson's choice saying, "You have to decide whether you want to stay with me or with mummy." In tears, Lennon initially chose his father but watching his mother turn and go was too much for him, and he ran after her, pleading that she not leave him. Julia took her son back to Liverpool, where her family decided he should be raised by her older sister Mimi.

So, it came to be that Lennon grew up in the home of Mary Elizabeth Smith (his Aunt Mimi and her husband, Uncle George). While Julia remained in his life, his aunt and uncle provided him with structure and care. The couple had no children of their own. It is not an understatement to say that both treasured the young Lennon. At the same time, it is equally accurate to state that the absence of parental love tugged and pulled at Lennon throughout his life.

From the time he entered school, Lennon excelled at art, and he was a ferocious reader. Even today, his classmates from his early days in primary school recall that he stuck out as somebody unusual or different. Some thought him odd and remembered that Lennon was usually involved if there were fights on the playground. Looking back on his early school days years later, Lennon said he thought he was either a genius or a madman. Of course, he added, that he knew he wasn't a madman.

When Lennon was 14, his uncle George died suddenly. Three years later, his mother was killed when a car went out of control and struck her as she was waiting at a bus stop. He got over his uncle's death in time, but his mother's loss would stay with him. Later he would write two very different songs about his mother. The hauntingly beautiful "Julia" that he recorded on the Beatles' *White Album*, and the searing song titled "Mother" appearing on his first solo effort.

Through movies like Rock Around the Clock and recordings by American artists like Elvis and Buddy Holly, Lennon's interest in Rock and Roll was first ignited. When he was unable to convince his aunt or his mother to buy him a guitar, he went the mail-order route and ordered one himself (Aunt Mimi would later buy him a better guitar, though she was quick to tell him that while playing it was all well and good, he'd never make a living that way). It didn't take Lennon long to form his first band, which he named the Quarrymen, taking the name from the Quarry Bank High School where he was a student. One of the band's early performances took place on July 6, 1957, and it is noteworthy as it was the day Lennon met Paul McCartney. A friend recalling that fateful day said the two "circled each other like cats."

As Lennon learned more about McCartney, one thing was evident to him. McCartney was a better musician. As the Quarrymen's leader, Lennon alone had the authority to choose who was in the group. Though he recognized that he was risking his authority, Lennon invited the 15-year-old McCartney to become a part of the band. In his excellent book *Lennon Revealed,* Larry Kane quotes Lennon, who stated, "I made a decision to have a better person in the group."

McCartney accepted the invitation and later spoke of his feelings at the time to Beatles biographer Hunter Davies. "I idolized John. He was the big kid in the chip shop. I was the little guy."

Meanwhile, back at Quarry Bank High School, the individualism that Lennon had exhibited in the primary grades had continued, except now he was viewed as a behavior problem. The teaching staff's general view was that he rebelled against any restraint or discipline. It was against this background that the school's headmaster sat down with Aunt Mimi to discuss Lennon's future after graduation. The headmaster suggested art college, and Mimi agreed, saying, "Any port in a storm." With the aid of the headmaster's recommendation, Lennon was accepted at the Liverpool College of Art.

It was in an art class that Lennon would meet Stuart Sutcliffe. Sutcliffe was a talented young artist who was a year ahead of Lennon at the school. By the time Lennon arrived at the art school, Sutcliffe's artistic talent had made him well known to the other students and teachers. Lennon sought him out, and the two became fast friends. If there was a peer that Lennon looked up to, it was Sutcliffe who, unlike the majority of his friends, was not afraid to hold Lennon responsible for his behavior. In speaking of Sutcliffe, Aunt Mimi said, "That was his only friend, he was the only other boy he really enjoyed being with for long periods of time." Yoko Ono, who never met Sutcliffe, said that Lennon had told her that he really cared for Sutcliffe and respected him as an artist.

In 1958, a friend of McCartney's named George Harrison joined the band, and in1960, Lennon brought Sutcliffe on board as the band's bass player. It was around this time that the Quarrymen changed their name to the Silver Beetles. By now, the group had five members with Pete Best working the drums. That August, the group played 48 straight nights at a club in Hamburg, Germany, as The Beatles.

By the time The Beatles arrived in Hamburg, Lennon had already flunked out of art college. Both Lennon and McCartney had begun writing songs. Some were written as a team and some individually, but the two agreed that whatever they wrote would be credited as a Lennon-McCartney composition. Also, the tension between McCartney and Sutcliffe was on the rise. For one thing, McCartney was jealous of the attention that Lennon gave Sutcliffe. Added to that was the fact that Sutcliffe was a gifted artist but not much of a musician. During the band's performances, he would turn his back to the audience to hide his ineptitude at playing the bass, which happened to be the instrument that McCartney wanted for himself. It was against this background that the group entered into what they would call the Hamburg Experience.

All told, The Beatles would make three trips to Hamburg as they honed their skills as a group with long non-stop performances and the beginning of their use of drugs, particularly uppers, to help them get through their shows. Among the German fans, they attracted was a beautiful photographer named Astrid Kirchherr. She is credited with creating The Beatle hairdo, and the first member of the band to wear it was Sutcliffe.

Kirchherr and Sutcliffe fell in love, and he decided to leave the group and stay in Germany to pursue his art. This decision depressed Lennon, though both McCartney and Harrison viewed the event favorably as it related to the group. Lennon's depression grew worse when Sutcliffe died on April 10, 1962, due to a cerebral hemorrhage. Kirchherr broke the news to Lennon as The Beatles arrived in Hamburg. She recalled that he reacted by bursting into hysterical laughter. In her view, it was his way of not having to face the truth. Lennon never forgot Sutcliffe, as evidenced by his dead friend's appearance on The Beatles' *Sergeant Pepper's* album cover.

Back in England, the band began making frequent appearances at Liverpool's Cavern Club. In all, they would make 292 appearances at the club. While they were working at the Cavern, The Beatles came to the attention of a local businessman named Brian Epstein. One day a customer walked into his shop and asked for a record *My Bonnie* by the Beatles. Epstein had never heard of it but promised to try and locate the recording. He made some inquiries and found that the group had recorded the song in Hamburg. He also found out that the same group on that record played in the Cavern Club, located a couple of football fields away from his shop.

Epstein took a trip to the club to see the group. He was captivated by their raw talent. He then arranged a few meetings with the boys, as he called them, where they discussed the future. Finally, Epstein told them they needed a manager, and he offered to do it. It was Lennon who accepted, saying, "Where's the contract? I'll sign it." On January 24, 1962, the others took pen in hand as well and signed on with Epstein for five years. That same year Lennon married his longtime girlfriend Cynthia Powell, who was pregnant with their first son, Julian.

Epstein never tried to influence The Beatles musically in any way. However, he did take charge in other ways. He set down rules that they take the stage on time, that eating and drinking during performances stop, and that there would be no yelling at the audience. The latter regulation was aimed directly at Lennon, who had taken to yelling insults at audiences during the Hamburg days. The Epstein decision that provoked the group's most significant debate occurred when he decided the band would wear suits and ties. It was an idea McCartney supported, and Lennon and Harrison fought. Even after the two gave in to Epstein's packaging plan, Lennon would appear onstage with his tie loosened and his top shirt button undone. It was his little rebellion.

With the packaging of his product complete, Epstein set about getting The Beatles a recording contract. In making the rounds, Epstein told people that The Beatles would be bigger than Elvis, but nobody was buying. Finally, he convinced E.M.I. to take a chance on the group. Before making their first record, The Beatles replaced their drummer. Pete Best was out, and Ringo Starr was in.

E.M.I. teamed The Beatles with producer George Martin. Martin's forte to that point had been classical music, a little pop but mainly comedy albums. When The Beatles arrived to make their first record with Martin, they only had a few original compositions. The band wanted to record the Lennon McCartney tune "Love Me Do," with which Martin wasn't impressed. He offered them other songs, but they wanted to do one of their own. So, "Love Me Do" it was. The record reached number

17 on the British charts. When Lennon played the record for his Aunt Mimi, she was unimpressed.

The Beatles then recorded a tune Lennon had written, which he said was inspired by Roy Orbison. Upon hearing the song, George Martin insisted that the band increase the tempo. When the recording was finished, Martin said, "Congratulations, gentlemen, you've just made your first number one record." When Lennon played it for Aunt Mimi, she told him, "That's more like it." "Please Please Me" did indeed rise to the top of the charts.

By 1963 Beatlemania had already engulfed England, and word of the band reached the United States. Contrary to popular belief, The Beatles' first American television appearance was not on the *Ed Sullivan Show* (see *Gotham Graves Volume One*, Chapter 23). A month before the Sullivan appearance, Jack Parr showed a film of The Beatles performing "She Loves You." After playing the film, Parr joked that it appeared that England had caught up to us culturally.

While it wasn't their first, The Beatles' February 1964 appearance on Sullivan's show was nothing short of historic. The four became international stars, led by the songwriting duo of Lennon and McCartney. The band ruled the pop charts for the remainder of the decade. Between 1964 and 1966, they made two successful movies. Lennon wrote two critically acclaimed books, and the band toured worldwide.

In 1966, just as The Beatles' last American tour was to begin, the United States magazine *Datebook* published a quote from an interview Lennon had given four months earlier. Lennon said, "Christianity will go, it will vanish and shrink. I needn't argue with that, I'm right, and I will be proved right. We're more popular than Jesus now; I don't know which will go first, rock and roll or Christianity. Jesus was alright, but his disciples were thick and ordinary. It's them twisting it that ruins it for me." Wire services picked it up, and in no time, there were headlines worldwide reporting that Lennon had said that The Beatles were more popular than Christ.

The reaction to the quote may have been most intense in the United States. Nearly 50 radio stations refused to play Beatle records. Rallies were held where teenagers were encouraged to toss Beatle records and memorabilia into bonfires. One can only imagine that had Christ been around, he might have said let he who has not sinned burn the first LP.

Epstein hurried to America to do damage control. Before leaving, he begged Lennon to issue a public apology, but Lennon refused, saying he had done nothing wrong. Only after being told that he was letting the band down did Lennon agree to go before the press in Chicago, where he said, "I apologize if it will make you happy. I still don't know what I've done." No doubt Epstein had hoped for more, but that was the best he was going to get.

Up to this point, there is little doubt that Lennon was the leader of the best-known band in the world. McCartney compared him to Elvis and said, "We all looked up to him." In his book, Larry Kane quotes The Beatles press officer, Tony Barrow, who said, "but the fact remains during the height of Beatlemania, John did the heavy lifting. When one of the boys was upset over something, Paul would go to John and complain. John would confront Brian. Brian would fix it or try to. And Paul would sometimes look like the good guy because he didn't want to engage in uncomfortable situations. Both were born leaders, but John was the risk-taker in dealing with heavy issues."

The Beatles gave their last full concert in San Francisco on August 29, 1966. Some believe the decision to stop touring was influenced by the band's death threats after Lennon's Christ comments. While that may have been a factor, the band's music's evolution certainly played a part. The Beatles abandoned the pop sound that had catapulted them to the top of the music world. Their recordings became more complicated, both musically and lyrically. While most of the songs were still credited to Lennon and McCartney (Harrison had begun writing), the two worked separately. Generally, whoever wrote the song was the lead vocalist. For example, McCartney was tugging at the heartstrings with songs like "Yesterday" and "Here, There and Everywhere." Lennon, heavily influenced by Bob Dylan, was penning "In My Life" and "Tomorrow Never Knows."

That November, Lennon went to London's Indica art gallery to view an exhibit by an avant-garde artist named Yoko Ono. The artist told

Lennon that he could climb a stepladder and hammer an imaginary nail into the wall for five shillings. Lennon responded that he would give her an imaginary five shillings to hammer the imaginary nail. Though they were both married, the two felt an immediate connection, and Lennon made it a point to stay in touch with Ono.

On June 1, 1967, The Beatles released the album *Sgt. Pepper's Lonely Hearts Club Band.* The recording met with immediate commercial and critical success. It would top the charts in both England and the United States for months. It was The Beatles' psychedelic masterpiece. Lennon, who, along with the other Beatles, was experimenting with LSD, wrote many memorable songs on the LP. These include "Lucy in the Sky with Diamonds" and, aside from McCartney's middle eight, "A Day in the Life." Decades later, *Rolling Stone* magazine would name *Sgt. Pepper's* the greatest album ever made.

Later Lennon would say that by this time, he was already growing tired of The Beatles. He was actively pursuing Yoko Ono though she initially showed little interest in a romantic relationship. A big blow came to the group on August 27, 1967, when Brian Epstein died from a drug overdose. According to his biographer, Ray Coleman, the death hit Lennon hard. Lennon said, "The Beatles were finished when Eppy died. I knew, deep inside me, that that was it. Without him, we'd had it."

McCartney moved in to fill the void left by Epstein's death. He came up with the idea to do a TV movie titled *The Magical Mystery Tour.* The film was shown on British TV on the day after Christmas in 1967. It was a critical disaster and constituted The Beatles' first failure. Lennon, whose attention had been diverted by Ono, participated half-heartedly in the project. He would later complain about the production cost, calling it the most expensive home movie ever made.

While The Beatles being finished may have been Lennon's view in retrospect, 1968 would prove to be a hectic year for both him and the band. In February, the group traveled to India to study transcendental meditation with Maharishi Mahesh Yogi. Lennon took his wife, Cynthia, on the trip, but he remained in contact with Ono through letters. In India, both Lennon and McCartney composed many of the songs on the album titled *The Beatles,* which came to be known as *The White Album.* Paul and Ringo were the first to tire of Maharishi and leave India. Lennon grew to find the man annoying, and he decided to leave as well. When Maharishi asked him why he was departing early, he said, "If you're so bloody cosmic, you'll know why."

Lennon had decided to end his marriage, and he and Cynthia were divorced that November. By this time, Lennon and Ono had already announced that she was pregnant with his baby. She would suffer a miscarriage that same month. While this was going on, The Beatles had formed the Apple Corporation, and the animated movie *Yellow Submarine* had been released. In August, the McCartney-composed "Hey Jude" climbed to the top of the record charts, where it stayed for nine weeks.

Lennon quickly grew disenchanted with Apple. One of its employees, Richard Dilello, would later write a book about the company describing it as an extended cocktail party. Lennon's concern was that through Apple, The Beatles were losing substantial amounts of money every month. The group held a meeting to discuss matters, and McCartney began suggesting that The Beatles perform live, perhaps at a Roman amphitheater or on a cruise ship. Lennon was having none of it and told the others that he was breaking up the group. While the albums *Abbey Road* and *Let It Be* were released later, for all intents and purposes, The Beatles broke up long before McCartney's official announcement on April 10, 1970. That announcement angered Lennon, who said, "I started the band. I disbanded it. It's as simple as that." He told *Rolling Stone,* "I was a fool not to do what Paul did, which was use it to sell a record." The comments started a public feud between the two that would explode in their music in the early '70s.

By the time McCartney made the split official, Lennon had already married Ono. The newlyweds made their honeymoon a peace event when they checked into an Amsterdam hotel and held a bed-in for peace. The couple knew that they would be covered by the press regardless of what they did, so they used the moment to promote a cause they both believed.

Lennon and Ono staged yet another bed-in in Montreal, Canada. A reporter asked Lennon what he was trying to accomplish through these antics. His response was, "Just give peace a chance." On June 1, 1969,

Lennon recorded the song with that title in the Queen Elizabeth Hotel room where he and Ono were staying. Though he was still technically a Beatle, he released it as a solo work. The song became an anthem of the American anti-war movement.

In December of 1969, Lennon organized a supergroup to perform at London's Lyceum Ballroom. The purpose of the show was to support the United Nations Children's Emergency Fund. He called the group the Plastic Ono Band, and it included George Harrison, Eric Clapton, Keith Moon, Billy Preston, and Klaus Voormann. During most of the performance, Ono sat at Lennon's feet, covered by a white bag.

In 1970, Lennon released his first solo album titled *John Lennon/ Plastic Ono Band*. The work received critical acclaim. Rock critic Greil Marcus said that Lennon's singing on the final verse of the song "God" "may be the finest in all of rock." The *Village Voice* named it the album of the year. Today it is considered by many to represent Lennon's finest solo work. In 2003 *Rolling Stone* placed it at number 22 in the magazine's listing of the 500 greatest albums ever made.

Lennon's next solo effort *Imagine* didn't receive his first album's critical praise, but it was a commercial success. Lennon left out what, to some, was offensive language so that the fans would listen to it. He said

Tribute to Lennon located in New York's Central Park.

the song "Imagine" was "Working Class Hero" with chocolate on it. The record did include a song directly aimed at McCartney titled "How Do You Sleep." A few months earlier, McCartney had written and recorded a song called "Too Many People." Lyrically McCartney's song took a shot at Lennon and his new lifestyle with the words:

> Too many people going underground
> Too many reaching for a piece of cake
> Too many people pulled and pushed around
> Too many waiting for that lucky break.
> That was your first mistake
> You took your lucky break and broke it in two
> Now what can be done for you
> You broke it in two.

Why McCartney chose to attack Lennon lyrically (when he above all people knew that was Lennon's strength) is anybody's guess. Lennon pulled no punches in his response:

> You live with straights who tell you you was king
> Jump when your momma tell you anything
> The only thing you done was yesterday
> And since you've gone you're just another day.
> How do you sleep?
> How do you sleep at Night?
>
> A pretty face may last a year or two
> But pretty soon they'll see what you can do
> The sound you make is musak to my ears
> You must have learned something in all those years.
> How do you sleep?
> How do you sleep at night?

Many thought the song "Crippled Inside" was also aimed at McCartney. Music fans followed the feud between the greatest songwriting team of their time with interest. As they say, time heals all wounds, and by the middle of the decade, the two had buried the hatchet and put their bad feelings behind them.

By 1971, Lennon and Ono had taken up residency in New York City. That December, the couple released their Christmas tune "Happy Xmas (War is Over)." The following year the Nixon administration, fueled by Lennon's anti-war and anti-administration political stances, took steps to deport the former Beatle. By March of 1972, Lennon had been ordered to get out of the country within two months. Lennon hired the attorney Leon Wildes to represent him in what would become a four-year battle. Throughout the conflict, Wildes successfully obtained extensions that allowed Lennon to stay in the United States. He was a prisoner of sorts since he knew that he wouldn't be permitted to return if he left the country.

Given the circumstances, one would think that Lennon would tread lightly when it came to political topics. That was hardly the case, as evidenced by the release of his next album, *Some Time in New York City*. The album was loaded with political statements from women's rights to England's presence and role in Northern Ireland's troubles. A single from the record "Woman is the Nigger of the World" was released but received very little radio airplay because of Lennon's use of the word "nigger." The album itself was a critical disaster. It was widely viewed as poorly written, and the backing band was viewed as mediocre at best.

At this point, Lennon and Ono were having relationship problems. In her view, she was pursuing her art while Lennon was partying into the wee hours. He had never been able to handle alcohol, and now he was doing a lot of drinking. Ono didn't want any part of the situation. While Lennon was working on his next record, Ono was deciding how to proceed. She decided that the two needed to be separated. Ono told John he had to leave and set him up with a female companion named May Pang. According to Larry Kane, Ono called Pang, who was working for the couple at the time, into her office and suggested that she'd be good for her husband. Though Pang was reluctant, Ono got her way, and Lennon and Pang began an affair. While the two were together, he released the album *Mind Games* near the end of 1973. While more successful than his previous LP, it was an inconsistent offering at best.

The year 1974 found Lennon and Pang heading to California for what became known as the "Lost Weekend." He continued his drinking, and his exploits with the singer Harry Nilsson were finding their way into the press. Two of the more publicized events took place at the Troubadour Club in Los Angeles. The one became known as the "Kotex Incident" when an intoxicated Lennon returned from the bathroom with a Kotex on his forehead. Seeing a waitress, he asked, "Don't you know who I am?"

She responded, ". . . some asshole with a Kotex on his head."

A few days later, Lennon and Nilsson were back at the same club to see the Smothers Brothers. Both men began drinking heavily, and Lennon began loudly heckling the performers. Peter Lawford, seated a few tables away, began yelling at Lennon to shut up. Ignoring Lawford, Lennon continued his harangue until bouncers removed both Lennon and Nilsson from the club.

Lennon and Pang headed back to New York, where they set up house together. That October, he released the album *Walls and Bridges.* Lennon produced the record himself, and it was a strong effort featuring quality songs like "Old Dirt Road" and "Nobody Loves You (When You're Down and Out)." The album's biggest hit was a sax-driven tune Lennon sang with Elton John titled "Whatever Gets You Through the Night." It became Lennon's only number one record as a solo artist. Elton John had bet Lennon that the song would reach number one and as payment Lennon agreed to appear with John at one of his live performances.

The two performed together on Thanksgiving Day, November 28, 1974. John tried to persuade Lennon to sing "Imagine," but Lennon refused, saying he didn't want to look like an old crooner doing his old hits. Instead, the two sang "I Saw Her Standing There," which Lennon introduced by saying it was written by an old fiancé of his, "Lucy in the Sky with Diamonds" and "Whatever Gets You Through the Night." The show was also noteworthy because it reunited Lennon and Yoko Ono, who met him backstage before the performance. Shortly after that, the two began living together again as man and wife.

In 1975 Lennon released the album *Rock and Roll.* While critics were unimpressed by the work, it does highlight Lennon's vocal talent.

New York's Strawberry Fields where fans gather to remember the man who brought The Beatles together.

Covering the hits when he was a boy, he does a great job on tunes like "Stand by Me" and "Rip It Up."

The rest of 1975 proved to be a banner year for Lennon. By October, he had won his immigration case and now had a green card. On the 9th of that month (Lennon's birthday), his second son, Sean, was born. A father again, Lennon devoted himself to raising Sean, saying, " we have basically decided, without any great decision, to be with our baby as much as we can until we feel we can take time off to indulge ourselves in creating things outside the family." True to his word Lennon became a house husband, and little was heard from or about him for the rest of the decade.

The retirement lasted until October 1980, when the single "(Just Like) Starting Over" was released. One month later, Lennon and Ono were back in the news with their new album *Double Fantasy*. Both the single and the album were big hits, and the two artists began planning a tour to place the following year.

On the night of December 8, 1980, Lennon and Ono returned to their apartment in New York's Dakota building just across the street from Central Park. As they were making their way into the building, a deranged

Lennon fan stepped from the shadows and began firing his gun. Four of the bullets struck Lennon, who fell at the entrance to the building. Lennon was rushed to a nearby hospital, but efforts to save him proved futile. He was pronounced dead at 11:07 P.M.

Lennon was cremated, and some believe that his ashes were scattered in New York's Central Park in the area now known as Strawberry Fields. There fans still gather to pay tribute to the memory of a man who became known for his honesty and humanity as much as for his talent. When we visited, we were surprised at the number of young people present, many of whom had to have been born after Lennon's untimely passing.

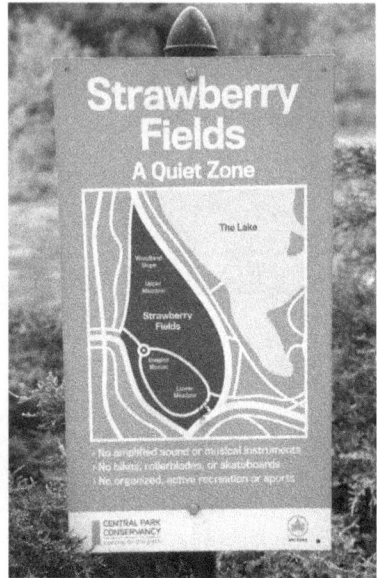

Not far from this quiet zone one can find street musicians remembering Lennon through his music.

Lennon has been honored numerous times since his death. For example, he has been inducted into the Rock and Roll Hall of Fame twice, once as a Beatle and once as a solo artist. Numerous artists have paid tribute to Lennon through their work, including George Harrison, Paul Simon, Joan Baez, Elton John, Queen, Bob Dylan, and yes, Paul McCartney. We like to believe that Lennon would have especially cherished his co-composer's effort.

If You Go:

The Imagine Memorial is in the Strawberry Fields section of Central Park across from Lennon's last home in the Dakota. You will undoubtedly run into many fans and a few musicians who gather daily to sing Lennon's compositions. You will also find street vendors selling Lennon related items like buttons and posters.

19

Bill "Bojangles" Robinson

"Mr. Bojangles"

County: Kings • City: Brooklyn
Buried at Cemetery of the Evergreens
4 Bushwick Avenue

Bill Robinson was an American tap dancer and actor, whose long career mirrored changes in American entertainment tastes, starting in the age of minstrel shows, moving to Vaudeville, Broadway, the recording industry, Hollywood, radio, and television. Some sources credit him for getting tap dance literally "up on its toes." Early forms of tap contained a flat-footed style, while Robinson performed on the balls of his feet, with a shuffle-tap style that allowed him more flexibility to improvise. The technique won him notice and eventually made him a legend.

Robinson was the best-known and most highly paid African American entertainer in the first half of the twentieth century. His signature routine was the stair dance, in which Robinson would tap up and down a set of stairs in a rhythmically complex sequence of steps. He refined the routine until it was one of the most spectacular events in the world of dance. He is best remembered for his dancing with Shirley Temple in a series of films during the 1930s and for starring in the musical *Stormy Weather* (1943).

He was born Luther Robinson in Richmond, Virginia, on May 25, 1878. He was orphaned when both his parents, Maria and Maxwell Robinson, died in 1885. His grandmother, Bedelia Robinson, subsequently reared him and his brothers. He disliked his birth name and suggested to his younger brother Bill that they should exchange names. Eventually, the exchange between brothers was made. The new "Luther" later adopted the name Percy and became a well-known drummer.

Mister Bojangles

At the age of five, Robinson began dancing for small change in local beer gardens and in front of theaters for tossed pennies. He claims this was when he picked up the nickname "Bojangles." A promoter saw him performing outside the Globe Theatre in Richmond and offered him a job as a "pick" in a local minstrel show. At that time, minstrel shows were staged by white performers in black face. Pickaninnies were cute black children at the edge of the stage, singing, dancing, or telling jokes. It is around this time that Robinson is said to have coined the phrase "everything's copacetic," meaning "fine, better than all right."

Robinson doing his famous stair dance.

At the age of thirteen, Robinson ran away to Washington, D.C., where he did odd jobs at Benning Race Track. He teamed up, at times, with Al Jolson, dancing for pennies while Jolson sang. He landed his first professional job in 1892 in Mayne Remington's *The South Before the War*, performing, again, as a pickaninny despite his age (14). He traveled with the show for over a year.

When the Spanish-American War broke out in 1898, 20-year-old Robinson joined the United States Army. He was a rifleman and was accidentally shot by an officer who was cleaning his gun.

By 1900, he had made his way to New York and rapidly rose to become one of America's best-loved nightclub and musical comedy performers. He was helped by his challenge to tap dancer Harry Swinton, the show's star dancer in *Old Kentucky*. The contest took place at Brooklyn's Bijou Theater on March 30, 1900, and Robinson won. The resulting publicity helped him get work in numerous shows, sometimes in a troupe, but more frequently with a partner, and not always as a dancer—Robinson also sang and performed two-man comedy routines.

He caught a break in 1902 when George W. Cooper replaced his vaudeville partner with Robinson. In 1903, the team, renamed "Cooper and Robinson," was signed by the B.F. Keith Circuit paid $100 per week and guaranteed 26 weeks (a big boost to Robinson's income). It was mostly a comedy act, with Robinson playing the buffoon to Cooper's straight man, and Robinson doing little dancing.

By 1912, Robinson was a full partner in the duo, and the show had become primarily a tap-dancing act booked on both the Keith and Orpheum Circuits, the two biggest at the time. The "two-colored" rule bound them in vaudeville, which restricted blacks to performing in pairs. The duo broke up in 1914, and vaudeville performer Rae Samuels, who had previously been in shows with Robinson, convinced him to meet with her husband and manager, Marty Forkins. Forkins got Robinson work as a solo act and made him one of the first performers to break the "two-colored" rule. Forkins managed to book him as a solo act at the Marigold Gardens Theater in Chicago. Robinson became one of the first black performers to headline at New York's prestigious Palace Theatre.

At the age of forty, Robinson served in World War I with New York's 15th Infantry Regiment, Army National Guard (later renamed the 369th Infantry), which earned the nickname "The Harlem Hellfighters." He received a commendation from the War Department, in 1918, for performing gratis for thousands of troops. Robinson was also the drum major who led the regimental band up Fifth Avenue upon the regiment's return from Europe.

After the war, and throughout most of the 1920s, Robinson toured the country as a solo vaudeville act. He did multiple shows per night, frequently at two different places.

Bill Robinson with Lena Horne and Cab Calloway.

In 1928, he starred on Broadway in the hugely successful musical revue, *Blackbirds of 1928*, which featured his famous "stair dance." It was produced by a white man, Lew Leslie, and was intended for white audiences. It starred black performers and ran to sell-out crowds for over a year. The show was a breakthrough for Robinson. He became well-known as "Bojangles," which connoted a cheerful and happy-go-lucky demeanor for his white fans, despite the opposite meaning in the black community.

His catchphrase "everything is copacetic" reinforced his supposed sunny disposition. The publicity that gradually came to surround Robinson included his gambling exploits, his bow ties of multiple colors, his generosity, his ability to run backward (he set a world's record of 13.5 seconds for the 100-yard backward dash in 1930, which remained the record until broken in 1977), and his love of ice cream.

After 1930, black revues waned in popularity, but Robinson's popularity endured. He starred in fourteen Hollywood motion pictures, many musicals and played multiple roles opposite child star, Shirley Temple. These films—including *Rebecca of Sunnybrook Farm, The Little Colonel,*

The Littlest Rebel, and *Just Around the Corner*—brought him the most fame. Rarely did he depart from the stereotype imposed by Hollywood writers. By accepting these roles, Robinson maintained steady employment and remained in the public eye.

He appeared opposite Will Rogers in the 1935 film *In Old Kentucky,* the last movie Rogers made before his airplane crash. They were good friends, and after Roger's death, Robinson refused to fly. He would travel by train.

His final film appearance was a starring role in the 1943 Fox musical *Stormy Weather.* Lena Horne was his co-star, and the movie featured Fats Waller and Cab Calloway and his orchestra. *Stormy Weather* was selected for preservation in the United States National Film Registry by the Library of Congress in 2001 as "culturally, historically or aesthetically significant."

In 1939, he returned to the stage in *The Hot Mikado,* a jazz version of the Gilbert and Sullivan operetta. It was a smash on Broadway and moved to the 1939 World's Fair, one of the fair's greatest hits. On August 25, 1939, "Bill Robinson Day" was celebrated at the fair.

From 1936 until he died in 1949, Robinson made numerous radio and television appearances. His appearances included dancing, but he also sang and told jokes and stories from his vaudeville days.

After appearing in *All in Fun* in 1940 (which failed to attract an audience), he confined himself to occasional performances. He publicly celebrated his 61st birthday by dancing down 61 blocks of Broadway backward, from Columbus Circle to 44th Street.

In Robinson's personal life, he was dogged by demons, enhanced by having to deal with the indignities of racism that limited his opportunities despite his great success. He had very little education and a nasty demeanor. He drank and gambled heavily and always carried a gold-plated pistol that he had a permit to carry. He loved to play pool and, at times, demanded silence when he had to make a shot. At the time, he would pull out his pistol, lay it on the edge of the pool table, and take his shot as the other patrons became quiet. Despite accounts of a quarrelsome and confrontational personality, his dancing was extraordinary. With little

Shirley Temple, his scenes were so endearing and legendary that is the way most people think of him.

Robinson was married three times, the first time to Lena Chase, in 1907. They separated in 1916 and divorced in 1922. His second wife was Fannie Clay, whom he married shortly after his divorce from Chase. That marriage ended in divorce in 1943. His third marriage was, in 1944, to Elaine Plaines. They remained together until his death. There were no children from any of the marriages.

He was a founding member of the Negro Actors Guild of America, performed in thousands of benefits throughout his career, and made generous contributions to charities and individuals. The haunting memories of surviving in the streets never left him.

After a series of heart attacks, he was advised to quit working. A few months later, on November 25, 1949, he died from heart failure at 71. Despite earning more than two million dollars during his lifetime, Robinson died penniless. Much of his wealth had gone to charities in Harlem before his death.

Robinson's funeral, arranged by longtime friend and television star Ed Sullivan (see *Gotham Graves Volume One*, Chapter 23), was held at the 369th Infantry Regiment Armory and attended by an estimated 32,000 people. Reverend Adam Clayton Powell, Sr. conducted the Abyssinian Baptist Church service, and New York Mayor William O'Dwyer gave the eulogy. He was buried at the Cemetery of the Evergreens in Brooklyn.

During his career, Robinson came under heavy criticism for playing stereotyped roles and took offense at such claims. Once, after being named as an Uncle Tom in the New York newspaper *The Age*, Robinson went to its office in Harlem, pistol in hand, demanding to see the editor. In his eulogy at Robinson's funeral, Powell argued against Robinson as an Uncle Tom figure, focusing on his ability to transcend color lines.

The 1968 folk song "Mr. Bojangles," which has been recorded by Harry Belafonte, Neil Diamond, Bob Dylan, Sammy Davis, Jr., and many others, was inspired by an obscure street performer. It has, however, passed into our folk culture as representing Robinson.

Here is the final resting place of the original Mr. Bojangles.

In 1973, Robinson's statue was erected in Richmond, Virginia, at the intersection of Adams and West Leigh Streets.

A biography, written by Jim Haskins and N.R. Mitgang was published in 1988, entitled *Mr. Bojangles: The Biography of Bill Robinson*.

In 1989, a joint Congressional resolution was passed establishing May 25 (Robinson's birthday) as National Tap Dance Day. In 1992, a park in Harlem was named in his honor.

A made-for-television film, entitled *Bojangles,* was released in 2001. The film earned Gregory Hines the NAACP Best Actor Award for his performance as Robinson. In 2002, he was inducted into the International Tap Dance Hall of Fame.

If You Go:

The Evergreens is the final resting place for over half-a-million people. It dates to 1849 and covers 225 acres.

Eight victims of the terrible Triangle Shirtwaist Factory Fire (1911) are buried there.

The Evergreens is also the final resting place for Charles Hoffman (1878–1930), a World War I double Medal-of-Honor recipient. His real name was Ernest Janson, but he served as "Charles Hoffman."

Also buried at The Evergreens is Amy Vanderbilt (1908–1974). Vanderbilt was an American authority on etiquette. In 1952, she published the best-selling book *Amy Vanderbilt's Complete Book of Etiquette,* which is still in circulation. She hosted radio and television programs about etiquette from 1954 to 1962. She died from injuries after falling or jumping out of a window in her Manhattan townhouse on December 27, 1974. It remains unclear whether her fall was accidental or suicide.

20

Fred Rogers

"America's Favorite Neighbor"

County: Westmoreland • Town: Latrobe
Buried at Unity Cemetery
114 Chapel Lane

Fred Rogers was an American treasure and icon. He had a profound effect on the lives of millions of people through his ministry to children and families. His message was simple; that you can be lovable just the way you are. He taught kindness and love over four decades through his television program, books, and songs. He helped children deal with common fears, such as starting school or going to the doctor. He became an American icon of children's entertainment and education as well as a symbol of compassion, patience, and morality. He received the Presidential Medal of Freedom, two Peabody Awards for his life's work, and was inducted into the Television Hall of Fame.

It all began in Latrobe, Pennsylvania, where Fred McFeely Rogers was born on March 20, 1928. He showed an early interest and aptitude for music fostered by his mother and maternal grandfather, Fred McFeely. He graduated from Latrobe High School and attended Dartmouth College before transferring to Rollins College in Florida, where he graduated with a degree in music in 1951.

He was fascinated with the new medium, television, so he put his plans to become a minister on a back burner and accepted a job with NBC in New York City. He worked on several shows but grew disillusioned and left to help found WQED, the nation's first community-supported public television station. He married his college sweetheart, Sara Joanne Byrd, moved back to the Pittsburgh area, and began working at WQED.

Fred Rogers

He developed *The Children's Corner,* a prototype for *Mister Rogers' Neighborhood* and, for the next several years, developed many of the puppets, characters, and music used in his later work, such as King Friday XIII, Daniel Striped Tiger, and X the Owl. During this time, Rogers was studying theology at nearby Pittsburgh Theological Seminary and was ordained a Presbyterian minister in 1962. That year he created a fifteen-minute version of *Mister Rogers' Neighborhood* for Canadian television, and in 1966, WQED launched the series as a half-hour show. In 1969, *Mister Rogers' Neighborhood* began airing on PBS stations across the United States.

Mister Rogers' Neighborhood was a carefully structured show. The routine of walking through the door and changing his sneakers and sweater was a ritual designed to give children a sense of security and to signal a time for a relaxed visit together. The trips between fantasy and reality had structured transitions, such as the summoning of the Neighborhood Trolley to take us from Mister Rogers's living room through a tunnel and into the Neighborhood of Make-Believe. Songs composed by Rogers, more than 200 in his career, were used to impart many of his messages through simple lyrics that speak to a child's concerns. Songs like Daniel Striped Tiger's "Sometimes I Wonder If I'm a Mistake" say it's okay for kids to be themselves, and "What Do You Do?" offers a list of ways for a child to deal with anger.

Typically, each week's episode explored a major theme, such as going to school for the first time or a visit to the hospital to show children what to expect. The program became a huge success. From 1968 to 1999, 895 episodes were produced, all of which Rogers wrote and executive produced. Often there were celebrity guests like Yo-Yo Ma, Tony Bennett, Julia Child, Lynn Swann, David Copperfield, and Pittsburgh native actor Michael Keaton who also worked on the show as a stagehand.

The popularity of the show and its repetitive format led to many parodies over the years. After Burger King used an actor impersonating Mister Rogers for a TV commercial ("Can you say, 'Flame-Broiled'? I knew you could"), Fred Rogers called the head of the company concerned that the ad was "confusing innocent children" into thinking he was promoting their fast-food franchises. Rogers never did any commercial promotions of any kind. Burger King openly apologized, and the commercial was pulled. Johnny Carson once did a skit on *The Tonight Show* called "Mister Rambo's Neighborhood." When Rogers complained, Carson apologized and expressed admiration for Rogers's work. Rogers did, however, have a good sense of humor and enjoyed Eddie Murphy's parody of his show on *Saturday Night Live* called "Mister Robinson's Neighborhood" ("Can you say, 'Eviction Notice'? I knew you could.")

Rogers also published many books to supplement the messages on his television show. Among these were *Mister Rogers Talks with Parents*,

You are Special, The World According to Mister Rogers, Important Things to Remember, and eight New Experiences titles such as *The New Baby, Moving*, and *When a Pet Dies*.

In 1968, Rogers was appointed Chairman of the Forum on Mass Media and Child Development of the White House Conference on Youth. In 1969 he appeared before the United States Senate in support of funding for PBS and the Corporation for Public Broadcasting. He spoke on the need for social and emotional education that public television provided and argued that alternative television programming helped encourage children to become happy and productive citizens, sometimes opposing fewer positive messages in the media and popular culture. He even recited lyrics to "What Do You Do?" The chairman of the subcommittee, Senator John Pastore, said the testimony had given him goosebumps. President Nixon had proposed cutting their budget to $9 million, but after Rogers's testimony, Congress agreed on $22 million.

In 1979, Rogers testified in the case *Sony Corp of America v. Universal City Studios Inc.* The Supreme Court considered his testimony and quoted him in the footnote in its decision that held that the Betamax video recorder did not infringe copyright.

At the 1998 Emmy's, Rogers was awarded the Lifetime Achievement Award. In accepting the award on stage, he said, "All of us have special ones who have loved us into being. Would you just take, along with me, ten seconds to think of the people who have helped you become who you are. Ten seconds of silence." The gesture brought many of the star-studded Hollywood crowd to tears and drew a standing ovation. After that, Rogers frequently repeated this in his many speeches and appearances.

Photo of Fred Rogers located at the Rogers Center on the campus of Saint Vincent's College in Latrobe.

This large statue of Fred Rogers sits just outside Heinz Field in Pittsburgh. The site is called Tribute to Children.

Production of *Mister Rogers' Neighborhood* ceased in December 1999 and the last week of original episodes aired in August 2000. After the production of the program ceased, Fred Rogers devoted his time to the *Mister Rogers' Neighborhood* website, writing books, and numerous speaking engagements.

Rogers was diagnosed with stomach cancer in December 2002. His last public appearance was as Grand Marshall of the Tournament of Roses Parade with Bill Cosby and Art Linkletter. He died on February 27, 2003, at his home with his wife by his side. He was just shy of 75 years old.

He never sought the spotlight, but the list of awards he was presented is enormous. The Presidential Medal of Freedom, the highest civilian award that can be bestowed, was awarded Rogers in 2002 by President George Bush. *Mister Rogers' Neighborhood* won four Emmy Awards, and Rogers was given a Lifetime Achievement Award by the Academy of Television Arts and Sciences. He was awarded two Peabody Awards, was named one of the "50 greatest TV stars of all time" by *TV Guide* in 1996, was inducted into the Television Hall of Fame in 1999, had an asteroid named after him (Misterrogers), and got a star on the Hollywood Walk of Fame. The Smithsonian Institution in Washington, D.C., has his signature sweater on display. There is a large memorial statue of Fred Rogers just outside of Heinz Field, and St. Vincent College in Latrobe is home to The Fred M. Rogers Center for Early Learning and Children's Media. In 2003, the U.S. House of Representatives unanimously passed Resolution 111 honoring Rogers for "his legendary service to the improvement of lives of children, his steadfast commitment to demonstrating the power of compassion, and his dedication to spreading kindness through example."

Fred Rogers was a soft-spoken man of great modesty with a steady hand and a generous heart. His television persona was no act. This author had the privilege of meeting him several times and even seeing him record an episode of *Mister Rogers' Neighborhood*. He was always patient, caring, humble, and kind to everyone. He is buried in historic Unity

Fred Rogers was laid to rest in this mausoleum in Latrobe, Pennsylvania.

Cemetery in Latrobe, Pennsylvania, in a mausoleum that does not bear his name. It has the name "Given," a relative of Rogers.

If You Go:

If you go to Latrobe, be sure to visit the beautiful, inspiring campus of the community of scholars known as St. Vincent College. Established in 1846, it has been turning out some of our best thinkers for over 150 years (This author went there). It's also the training camp of the Pittsburgh Steelers. If that's not enough stimulation, stop at Sharky's Café at 3960 Rt 30. Sharky's has been turning out some of our best drinkers for many years. It's the area's largest and most complete restaurant and sports bar. Even President Obama and Senator Bob Casey stopped in for a beer when campaigning in the area. It's a festive, friendly atmosphere. We loved it.

21

Lillian Russell

"The Great American Beauty"

County: Allegheny • Town: Pittsburgh
Buried at Allegheny Cemetery
4734 Butler Street

She was one of the most famous entertainers of the late 19th and early 20th centuries. She was known for her acting and singing. She was admired for her beauty as well as her stage presence. She was married four times, with her longest relationship being with Diamond Jim Brady, who allowed her to live the lifestyle she had grown accustomed to for four decades. She was often referred to as the most beautiful woman in the world. Her name was Lillian Russell.

Russell was born in Clinton, Iowa, on December 4, 1860. Shortly after her birth, her parents moved to Chicago, where she was raised. Her father, Charles Leonard, was a newspaper publisher. Her mother was a noted feminist named Cynthia Leonard, who would become the first woman to run for mayor of New York City. Growing up in Chicago, she appeared in many school productions. Also, she began to study music on her own, and she sang in choirs.

When she was eighteen, her parents separated, and Russell moved with her mother to New York. Soon after settling in New York, she joined the chorus of the Brooklyn Park Theatre. She was also taking singing lessons during this period. In 1879, she made her initial appearance on Broadway at Tony Pastor's Theatre, where she was billed as an "English ballad singer." Pastor, whom many credit with being the founder of vaudeville, was known for recognizing and introducing new performers. It was Pastor who gave her a new name and set her on the path to becoming a star.

Lillian Russell

Later in 1879, she joined the touring production of Gilbert and Sullivan's *H.M.S. Pinafore*. Within two weeks, she married the company's orchestra director Harry Braham after she discovered she was pregnant. She gave birth to a son who died when a nanny who was changing a diaper pierced the baby's stomach with a pin. The marriage dissolved soon after.

By 1881, she was back in Pastor's Theatre, where she had a role as the leading soprano in a burlesque of the *Pirates of Penzance*. During this period, she appeared in several New York theatres. It was at the Casino Theatre in 1883 that she met the composer Edward Solomon while she

1882 photo of Lillian Russell in the Bijou Opera House production of Gilbert and Sullivan's Patience.

was starring in a play called *Billee Taylor*. In 1884 Russell and Solomon were wed about one year after the birth of their daughter, who was named Dorothy Lillian Russell.

She traveled with Solomon to England, where she appeared in several of his productions, including *Pocahontas* and *Polly*. She was in London when she was hired to play the title role of Princess Ida in a Gilbert and Sullivan production. However, during rehearsals, she had disagreements with Gilbert, and he dismissed her. She returned to the States and went on tour for Pastor appearing in comic operas that were composed by her husband. Solomon was arrested for bigamy in 1886 since when he had married Russell, he had not yet obtained a divorce from a previous marriage. Russell divorced Solomon in 1893. During this period, Russell was also the companion of Diamond Jim Brady, who loved her. For forty years, he would present her with diamonds and other gems while he supported her luxurious lifestyle.

Russell had become the most famous singer of operettas in the country. The news media touted her singing ability as well as her beauty and stage presence. The actress Marie Dressler once said of Russell, "I can still recall the rush of pure awe that marked her entrance on the stage. And then the thunderous applause that swept from orchestra to gallery, to the very roof."

It was the inventor of the telephone, Alexander Graham Bell, who introduced long-distance calling in 1890. Russell singing the "Sabre Song" to listeners in Boston and Washington, D.C., was the first voice heard over those telephone lines. For fun, during this time frame, she and her friend Diamond Jim Brady would ride bikes together in Central Park. Russell's bike had been made for her by Tiffany and Company. It was a gold-plated bike set with diamonds and emeralds. The bike cost $1,900.

From 1899 to 1904, Russell starred for the Weber and Fields Music Hall. In 1902 before the production of *Twirly-Whirly,* John Stromberg, who had already composed several hit songs for Russell, was slow in delivering her solo for the show giving the excuse that it simply wasn't ready. A few days before the rehearsals were to begin, Stromberg committed suicide. A song titled "Come Down My Evening Star" was found in one of his pockets. It would become Russell's signature song and the only one she ever recorded. She would take her place on stage in a $3,900 diamond-studded corset and deliver the number. At the time, she was being paid $5,000 per week.

After leaving Weber and Fields, Russell made numerous appearances on vaudeville stages. Around this time, she began having vocal problems, so she started appearing in non-musical comedies. She did so until 1911, when she returned to singing in burlesque and variety theatres.

Lillian Russell

In 1912, Russell married for the fourth time. Her husband, Alexander Pollock Moore, was the owner of the *Pittsburgh Leader*. After her marriage, she seldom appeared on stage, entering a semi-retirement stage.

That same year she made her last appearance on Broadway. In 1915, she appeared in the film *Wildfire,* which also starred Lionel Barrymore. She made her last appearance on the vaudeville stage in 1919. Ill health forced her to retire after a career that spanned four decades.

Here's the final resting place for a woman considered to be one of the great beauty's of her time.

After retiring from the stage, Russell wrote a newspaper column and was a strong supporter of women's rights as her mother had been. During World War 1, she aided the Marines in their recruiting efforts. By this time, she was a very wealthy woman, and she made a sizable donation to sponsor the formation of a Chorus Equity Association for the chorus girls of the Ziegfeld Follies.

On September 21, 1919, the *Gettysburg Times* reported Russell's car had broken down near the town while passing through from Pittsburgh to Atlantic City. It was Plank's Garage, owned by former baseball pitcher Eddie Plank, that came to the rescue.

In 1922, President Harding sent Russell to Europe on a fact-finding mission to investigate the increase in immigration to the United States. She recommended a five-year moratorium on immigration, and some of her findings found their way into the 1924 immigration reform law. On the return trip, she suffered minor injuries, which led to complications, and she died at her home in Pittsburgh ten days after her return on June 6, 1922. She was 61 years old, and she was laid to rest in Allegheny Cemetery in Pittsburgh.

If You Go:

You could spend all day touring Allegheny Cemetery. Among the people interred there are the legendary baseball player Josh Gibson, the noted composer Stephen Foster, and Harry Thaw, whose story was included in the book and movie *Ragtime* (All three have chapters in *Keystone Tombstone Volume Two*). The great jazz saxophonist Stanley Turrentine's final resting place is here as well.

There are two Civil War Medal of Honor recipients, Archibald H. Rowland Jr. and Alfred L. Pearson, buried here as well. After the war, Pearson commanded the National Guardsmen who were sent to Luzerne County to quell riots in the coal region. He ordered his men to open fire on the rioters and killed several of them. As a result, he was arrested and charged with murder, but a grand jury failed to indict him, and he was set free.

Also, you may want to visit the Arsenal Monument, which is also on the cemetery grounds. The monument honors 43 women who are buried here after an explosion at the nearby Allegheny Arsenal took their lives. The explosion was the worst industrial accident associated with the Civil War.

Not far from the cemetery, there is a great restaurant called Piccolo Forno. It is located at 3801 Butler Street. The eatery offers great service and terrific Italian food that is reasonably priced. It's worth checking out.

22

Soupy Sales

"A Pie in the Face™"

County: Westchester • Town: Valhalla
Buried at Kensico Cemetery
273 Lakeview Avenue

When you hear about Soupy Sales' early life, you suspect it's one of his numerous pranks. He was born Milton Supman in Franklinton, North Carolina, to Irving and Sadie Supman, the only Jewish family in town. He was born on January 28, 1926, and had two brothers, Leonard and Jack. The family name was often mispronounced as "Soupman" and his parents had nicknamed his brothers "Hambone" and "Chicken Bone." They gave Milton the nickname "Soupbone," which eventually became just "Soupy."

Sales' father ran a dry goods store in Franklinton, and Soupy often joked that local Ku Klux Klan members bought their sheets from his father's store. His father died when he was five, and the family moved to Huntington, West Virginia. Soupy acted in school plays and was voted the most popular boy. He graduated in 1944 from Huntington High School and enlisted in the United States Navy, where he served on the USS *Randall* in the South Pacific during World War II. He sometimes entertained his shipmates by telling jokes and playing crazy characters over the ship's public address system. One of the characters he created was "White Fang," a large dog that played outrageous jokes on the seamen. Surely the humor was a blessing as the USS *Randall* navigated the South Pacific and participated in the Battle of Okinawa.

After the war, Sales returned home and entered Marshall College to study journalism. While attending Marshall, he performed in nightclubs

Soupy Sales

as a comedian, singer, and dancer. He graduated in 1949 and went to
work for a radio station in Huntington as a scriptwriter, while he continued to do stand-up comedy in nightclubs and worked as a disc jockey.
Later that year, he moved to Cincinnati to work as a morning deejay. He
developed the stage name "Soupy Hines." Later he would change the
"Hines," deciding it was too close to Heinz Soup Company, to "Sales" in
honor of Chic Sale, a vaudeville comedian of some note. In Cincinnati,

Sales began his television career on WKRC-TV with a show called *Soupy's Soda Shop*. It was the first teenage dance television show program, beating Dick Clark's *American Bandstand* by two years. He also had a late-night comedy/variety program called *Club Nothing*.

After a couple of years, WKRC canceled his shows, and Sales moved to Cleveland, where he hosted radio and TV shows and continued his nightclub act. The late-night comedy/variety show was called *Soupy's On*, and it was a skit on that show where he got his first pie in the face.

In 1953, Sales left Cleveland "for health reasons" (he claimed "they got sick of me") and moved to Detroit for a job with WXYZ-TV. He launched a daily live children's show called *Soupy Sales Comics*, which caught on and led to his nighttime show *Soupy's On*. In 1955, the noontime show's name was changed to *Lunch with Soupy*, and it began to be broadcast nationally on the ABC television network. He hosted 11 hours of TV time each week, and *Lunch with Soupy* was the first non-cartoon Saturday morning program on the ABC network. The show was improvised and slapstick in nature, full of comedy sketches, gags, and puns, almost all of which resulted in Sales receiving a pie in the face, which became his trademark.

Sales developed pie-throwing into an art form. He took pies from all angles and multiple pies in rapid succession and countless variations. He bantered with stagehands and with a gallery of puppets that included Pookie (a hipster lion), White Fang ("the meanest dog in the United States") who only grunted expressively and was seen as just a large furry paw, and Black Tooth ("the biggest and sweetest dog in the United States") who also was a furry paw that gave Sales slurpy off-screen kisses. Other characters included his irrepressible girlfriend Peaches, the vivacious Marilyn Monwolf, and a bloodthirsty neighbor, the Count, who touted an album titled "Love in Vein."

Guest stars like Frank Sinatra, Burt Lancaster, Shirley MacLaine, and Sammy Davis, Jr. would come on the show and get plastered with a pie in the face. One show featured Sinatra, Sammy Davis, Jr., and Trini Lopez, all getting pied together. While meant for kids, the show developed a cult following among adults. Meanwhile, *Soup's On* was thriving on its

If you were close to Soupy you were in danger of taking one to the face.

own. It was on at 11 o'clock, and the guest star was always a musician (frequently a jazz musician). His show seemed to help sustain jazz in Detroit as artists would regularly sell out their club shows after appearing on *Soup's On*. Coleman Hawkins, Louis Armstrong, Duke Ellington, Billie Holiday, Charlie Parker, and Stan Getz were among the guests on the show, and Miles Davis made six appearances.

In 1960, Sales moved his show to the ABC-TV Studios in Los Angeles. However, ABC dropped the show from the network schedule in March 1961 while continuing the series as a local program until January 1962. The show went back on the network as a late-night fill-in for *The Steve Allen Show* in 1962 but was canceled after only three months.

During this time in Los Angeles, Sales started a sporadic film career that lasted more than 40 years. His movie debut was in *The Two Little Bears* (1961), which starred Eddie Albert, Jane Wyatt, and Nancy Kulp. He made his debut in a starring role in 1966 in *Birds Do It*, which also starred Tab Hunter and Arthur O'Connell. His last movie was *Angels with Angles* in 2005, in which he appeared with Frank Gorshin, Rodney Dangerfield, and Adam West.

In September 1964, Sales took his show to WNEW-TV in New York City, where it soon became the biggest show of its kind in local television. Screen Gems syndicated 263 episodes, and soon the show was seen throughout the U.S., Canada, Australia, and New Zealand. This show marked the height of his popularity. He was able to attract guest appearances by stars such as Frank Sinatra, Tony Curtis, Jerry Lewis, Sammy Davis, Jr., Judy Garland, and musical acts like The Shangri-Las, The Supremes, and The Temptations. Sales performed musical numbers on the show, often using his jazz collection

Soupy during his heyday.

and adapted popular jazz numbers as themes for his puppet characters. Frank Nastasi played White Fang, Black Tooth, Pookie, and all the "guy at the door" characters.

For notoriety, nothing beat the show that aired live on January 1, 1965. Sales was somewhat miffed at working on New Year's Day and had a few minutes to kill at the end of his program. Ad-libbing, Sales looked into the camera and delivered a request to his young viewers to sneak some "little green pieces of paper" out of their parents' wallets and send them to him. (No tape of the show exists, so a verbatim transcription of what Sales said is not available.) Complaints from outraged parents came fast and furious. Sales' show was suspended, prompting fans to swamp the station's switchboard with protest calls, mostly from high school and college students who demanded that Soupy be put back on. Within two weeks, he was. The uproar only increased his popularity. Sales described the incident in his autobiography *Soupy Sez! My Life and Zany Times* (2001).

Later that year, Sales invented a dance called The Mouse, a loony version of The Twist in which Sales bared his upper teeth, raised his hands to his ears, and wiggled his fingers while chewing in time to the music. He performed The Mouse on the *Ed Sullivan Show* in September 1965, just before The Beatles' segment of the broadcast (which would turn out to be the band's last live appearance on the show). While appearing on the Sullivan show, he met dancer Trudy Carson and married her in 1980 (less than a year after he and his first wife, Barbara Fox, got divorced after 29 years of marriage).

In the late '60s, animation took over children's programming, and shows like Sales' and Shari Lewis' lost their appeal. In 1966, his show was not renewed in New York and went into syndication. The show did make a brief comeback as *The New Soupy Sales Show* in 1978 in Los Angeles. It ran for one season live and then was syndicated.

One of Sales' biggest fans was Frank Sinatra. When Sinatra started his record label, Reprise Records, he signed Sales to a recording contract for which Sales produced two albums: *The Soupy Sales Show* in 1961 and *Up in the Air* in 1962. He also recorded a single—"Muck-Arty Park" (a play on "MacArthur Park")—and an album, *A Bag of Soup*, for Motown Records in 1969.

Soupy Sales was everywhere. He did Broadway, dinner theater, comedy clubs, loads of radio, television, and film. In 1968 he joined the panel on *What's My Line?* and went on to record 1,500 shows in his seven-year run. He was also a panelist on the revival of *To Tell the Truth*, and a frequent guest on *Match Game, The Gong Show, Hollywood Squares,* and *Pyramid,* as well as a featured performer in the musical variety show *Sha Na Na.*

For two years in the mid-'80s, Sales emceed a radio show on WNBC in New York, sandwiched between the drive-time shows of Don Imus in

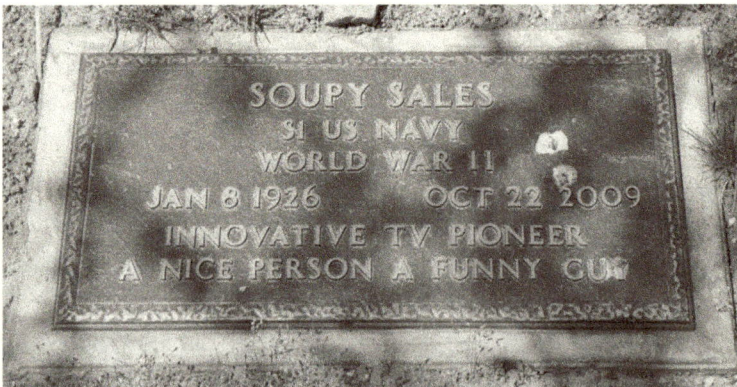

The modest grave of a funny man.

the morning and Howard Stern in the afternoon. The relationship between them was rocky. Stern and Imus gave Sales a hard time. After Sales
died, Stern admitted it on the air and claims he apologized to Sales some
years before his death. He praised Sales, claiming he was his childhood
hero and expressed regret over his harsh words towards Soupy. When
Sales' show was not renewed in 1987, he lost his temper on the air and
began to speak frankly about how he had been treated poorly by the
station. When the show went to commercial, Sales was off the air and
never returned.

Sales kept up club appearances through the 1990s, remaining popular
with baby boomers. He died of cancer on October 22, 2009, at Calvary
Hospice in the Bronx at 83. He is buried in a modest grave at Kensico
Cemetery in Valhalla, New York.

If You Go:

Kensico is a large, beautiful cemetery containing many notable graves,
including Anne Bancroft (1931–2005) (see *Gotham Graves Volume One*,
Chapter 2), Lou Gehrig (1903–1941), and Danny Kaye (1911–1987).

Two other notable graves at Kensico are David Sarnoff's (1891–1971)
and Florenz Ziegfeld (1867–1932).

Sarnoff was an American businessman and pioneer of American radio
and television. He was the founder of NBC and led RCA from its founding in 1919 until his retirement in 1970. At the onset of World War II,
Sarnoff served on Eisenhower's communications staff, and in December
1945, he received a brigadier general's star and, after that, was known
as General Sarnoff. The star which he proudly and frequently wore was
buried with him. He died the year after he retired at the age of 80.

Ziegfeld—popularly known as "Flo"—was an American Broadway
impresario, notable for his series of theatrical revues, the Ziegfeld Follies,
and his production of the musical *Show Boat*. He is a member of the
American Theater Hall of Fame. The Follies featured many famous
names such as Fanny Brice, W.C. Fields, and Will Rogers. Ziegfeld died
in 1932 at the age of 65.

23

Jean Stapleton

"The Dingbat"

County: Franklin • Town: Chambersburg
Cremated

Jean Stapleton was a well-known American actress known for her character roles on stage, screen, and television. She remains unforgettable among
television audiences for her portrayal of Edith Bunker on the highly
successful, groundbreaking situation comedy *All in the Family*. This role
won her eight Emmy nominations (three wins) and seven Golden Globe
nominations (two wins), making her a symbol of emergent feminism
in American popular culture. A trained singer, she appeared in musicals
both on and off Broadway, appeared in numerous non-musical plays,
and received both Emmy and Golden Globe nominations for the roles
of Eleanor Roosevelt in the TV movies *Eleanor, First Lady of the World*
(1982) and Aunt Vivian in *Grace Under Fire* (1994). She also appeared
in twelve Hollywood movies, from *Damn Yankees* (1958) to *Pursuit of
Happiness* (2001).

She was born Jeanne Murray on January 19, 1923, in Manhattan. Her
mom, Marie Stapleton, was an opera singer, and her dad, Joseph Murray,
was a billboard advertising salesman. She graduated from Wadleigh High
School at sixteen and started at Hunter College. She soon got interested
in acting, quit college, and learned secretarial skills to support herself
while studying and performing with the American Actors Company.

She started her career in 1941 with summer stock theater at the
Greenwood Gardens Playhouse in Peaks Island, Maine. There she chose
Stapleton as her as her stage name. She made her New York debut in
November 1953, but before that, she toured nationally in *Harvey* and as

Jean Stapleton

Shirley Booth's understudy in *Come Back Little Sheba*. She then opened off-Broadway in *American Gothic*. Soon after, she made her Broadway debut in *In the Summer House*.

Her performance opened doors to television series, and she made appearances on *Starlight Theater*, *Robert Montgomery Presents*, the *Philco-Goodyear Television Playhouse*, and the daytime drama *Woman with a Past*. Then in 1955, she landed a part in the original cast of *Damn Yankees*, where she sang the hit song "You Gotta Have Heart." A year later, she starred in another hit musical, *Bells Are Ringing*.

In 1958 and 1960, those two shows were made into films, and Stapleton reprised both her roles. In 1957, during the run of *Bells Are Ringing*, she married Bill Putch, who directed a summer stock theater, Totem Pole Playhouse, in Fayetteville, Pennsylvania. They were married until Putch died in 1983. They had two children. Stapleton performed there nearly every summer for 25 years. She was featured on Broadway fairly steadily for the next few years, including performing with Barbra Streisand in *Funny Girl*. She also did non-musicals such as Eugene Ionesco's *Rhinoceros* (1961).

The sixties found Stapleton heavily involved in television. She had guest roles in dozens of shows; among them were *The Naked City*, *Dr. Kildare*, *Dennis the Menace*, *My Three Sons*, *The Patty Duke Show*, and *The Defenders*, where she worked with an obscure actor named Carroll O'Connor (1962). She also appeared in the films *Something Wild* (1961), *Up the Down Staircase* (1967), *Klute* (1971), and the Norman Lear comedy *Cold Turkey* (1971) with Bob Newhart and Dick Van Dyke.

Norman Lear was a budding producer and, in 1968, was attempting to adapt a British comedy series *Till Death Do Us Part* for an American audience. He chose Stapleton to play Edith Bunker. Two pilots made in 1968 and 1969 failed to win the approval of ABC executives, but CBS picked up the third pilot. At first, the ratings were not promising, but the show won several Emmy Awards and gained popularity in summer reruns. One of the Emmys was won by Stapleton, besting Mary Tyler Moore and Marlo Thomas for "Best Actress in a Comedy."

It was the top-rated television show in its second season, and it remained at the top for five years. The role earned her three Emmys and two Golden Globes. The series ran from 1971 to 1979 and was followed by *Archie Bunker's Place*. Stapleton, however, requested to be written out of the show, as she had tired of the role. In the first episode of season two, Edith was written out via a stroke.

In 1977 Stapleton was appointed by President Jimmy Carter to the National Commission on the Observance of International Women's

Year. The Commission organized the National Women's Conference in Houston, Texas, gathering 2,000 delegates from all fifty states to formulate a national policy on women's rights.

Stapleton took on roles that were starkly different from Edith Bunker after leaving the Bunker household. She had no trouble shaking off Edith. "When you finish a role, you're done with it. There's no deep spooky connection with the parts you play," she told the AP in 2002.

In 1982 Stapleton portrayed Eleanor Roosevelt in the TV movie *Eleanor, First Lady of the World*, focusing on the subject's later life. Her performance earned her both Emmy and Golden Globe Award nominations.

The next year, while on tour with a play directed by her husband William Putch, he suffered a fatal heart attack at 60. She went on stage in Syracuse, New York, that night and continued with the tour. "That's what he would have wanted," she told *People Magazine*.

During the '80s, Stapleton remained very busy in television, film, and theater. She appeared in episodes of *Faerie Tale Theater*, *Scarecrow and Mrs. King*, and *The Love Boat*, among many others. She was in the TV movies *Something's Afoot*, *A Matter of Sex*, and *Dead Man's Folly*, among others, and in 1980 won two Obie awards for her performances off-Broadway in Harold Pinter's *The Birthday Party* and *Mountain Language*.

In 1990 and 1991, Stapleton co-starred with Whoopi Goldberg in fifteen episodes of *Bagdad Café*, the television series based on the movie of the same name.

In 1992 she was nominated for a Golden Globe Award for Best Supporting Actress for her role in *Fire in the Dark*, a television movie with Olympia Dukakis and Edward Herman. Another Emmy nomination in 1994 for an appearance on *Grace Under Fire*, and in 1996, she appeared on two hit television shows, *Everybody Loves Raymond* and *Murphy Brown*. During this period, the feature films she made include *Michael* opposite John Travolta and *You've Got Mail* with Meg Ryan and Tom Hanks. Her last film was in 2001 in *Pursuit of Happiness*. She was inducted into the American Theater Hall of Fame in 2002 and the Television Hall of Fame that same year.

Stapleton's husband's grave in Chambersburg

Stapleton died at her apartment in Manhattan on May 31, 2013, at age 90. Several sources claim she was buried in Lincoln Cemetery in Chambersburg, but that is apparently untrue. According to the staff at the cemetery, her husband is buried there, but they claim no knowledge of her remains. Other sources claim she was cremated, and her ashes were spread on her husband's grave and at Totem Pole Playhouse.

24

Sister Rosetta Tharpe

"The Godmother of Rock and Roll"

County: Philadelphia • Town: Philadelphia
Buried at Northwood Cemetery
1501 Haines Street

Her gospel recordings in the 1930s and '40s made her a star. She was a singer, a songwriter, and a guitarist. When it came to playing the electric guitar, she was a pioneer. Her use of heavy distortion and her guitar playing technique influenced the British blues movement in the 1960s. Eric Clapton, Keith Richards, and Jeff Beck are among those that took notice of her talents. The early rock and roll American musicians she influenced include Chuck Berry, Little Richard, Johnny Cash, and Elvis. She has been called the first soul sister and the godmother of rock and roll. In 2018 she was inducted into the Rock and Roll Hall of Fame. Her name was Sister Rosetta Tharpe.

She was born Rosetta Harper on March 20, 1915, in Cotton Plant, Arkansas. Her mother's name was Katie Bell Harper, and her father was Willis or Willie Atkins. Bother parents were cotton pickers. Very little is known about her father aside from the fact that he was a singer. Her mother, who was also a singer and a musician, would profoundly influence her daughter for the duration of her life.

Tharpe's parents were members of the Church of God in Christ (COGIC). Gayle F. Wald in her Tharpe biography *Shout, Sister, Shout!* describes the religious services in the church as exciting and dramatic. There was plenty of lively music during these events, which featured both singing and dancing. It was at these services that Tharpe was initially introduced to religious songs. COGIC also permitted the congregation

Rosetta Tharpe

to participate using musical instruments, including drums and guitars. In addition, the music, although faith-based, included elements of the blues and ragtime. The idea was that those musical forms encouraged those in attendance to move their bodies and engage in "holy dancing." The sermons during these gatherings generally included dreadful descriptions of hell and beautiful visions of heaven.

With the encouragement of her mother, Tharpe, at the age of four, began singing and playing the guitar at the church services. By the time she was six, she had joined her mother as a performer in an evangelical touring show. The young girl was billed as a "singing and guitar playing miracle." As the troupe toured the south, Tharpe was seen as a musical prodigy.

In the early 1920s, Tharpe and her mother moved to Chicago; Tharpe's father did not accompany them. The Roberts Temple COGIC, located on 40th Street, was the largest church of its kind in the Windy City. When Tharpe and her mother became members, they may well have joined the largest COGIC congregation in the United States. The Reverend Roberts also was liberal in the use of music during church services. This certainly contributed to Tharpe's musical development. On Sunday mornings, the church would be filled with loud singing accompanied by all types of instruments, including trumpets and trombones, if they were available. Tharpe and her mother performed religious concerts at the church. As detailed in *Shout, Sister, Shout*, a member of the congregation that attended these concerts, later described the young girl's performance, "It was just her singing, and her picking of the guitar that just drew. You just got attached to it. You can sing, and it's a beautiful voice and everything, but if you sing with an understanding and the feeling of what you're singing, it's altogether different. And that is what she did, more like to me. Even though she was young, it was a gift. Yes."

Word spread around Chicago about the talented young girl. Soon people from other churches began coming to see her. By this time, Tharpe was also providing her mother with financial assistance. After she performed, a collection was taken, and it was understood that it was going to her.

By the end of the 1920s, Tharpe and her mother began traveling and performing outside the northern Midwest. Tharpe honed her musical skills in the decade that followed by appearing at revivals and tent meetings. According to her biographer, it was during this time she also developed showmanship. When singing, she would improvise lyrics which became one of her trademarks.

Tharpe and her mother continued to travel during her late teenage years. During these travels, she met a COGIC preacher named Thomas J. Tharpe, and on November 17, 1934, the couple was married in Chicago. Not much is known about her first husband except that he traveled with his wife and her mother and would preach at their performances. In 1938 she left her husband and moved to New York with her mother.

Even though she would marry several more times, she kept her first husband's surname and would perform as Sister Rosetta Tharpe for the rest of her life.

Tharpe left more than her husband in 1938. She also decided to leave the church and pursue a secular career. When church members heard about Tharpe, the news was that she was now Sister Rosetta Tharpe, a Decca recording artist. In New York, she was no longer performing at a COGIC church but New York's famous Cotton Club. The club had an admission policy that allowed no blacks except for visiting entertainers seated in the rear. The club's audience generally included the nation's elite. For example, in 1939, those seated in front of Tharpe during the fall review included J. Edgar Hoover, Mary Martin, and the president of Universal Pictures, Nate Blumberg.

Tharpe was 23 in 1938 when she made her first recordings for Decca, backed by a jazz orchestra. These first gospel songs released by Decca became instant hits. Tharpe instantly became one of the first commercially successful gospel recording artists. These recordings included the song *Rock Me*, which influenced several early rockers, including Elvis, Little Richard, and Jerry Lee Lewis.

On December 23, 1938, Tharpe performed in John Hammond's *Spirituals to Swing* concert at Carnegie Hall. This increased both her fame and her notoriety. It was uncommon for a performer to entertain an audience singing gospel music for nightclub audiences along with musicians versed in blues and jazz and scantily clad chorus girls. A woman playing the guitar in these venues was met with disapproval among conservative churchgoers, and Tharpe fell out of favor with some parts of the gospel community. Still, as noted in her biography, her performance was a triumph. Count Basie, who appeared that night, recalled, "She sang some gospel songs that brought the house down. She sang down-home church numbers and had those old cool New Yorkers shouting in the aisles. There were a lot of people out there who had never heard that kind of singing, but she went over big."

During these years, excellent guitar skills were generally associated with male musicians. Tharpe would participate in guitar battles with these musicians at Harlem's Apollo Theater. She was soon having her skills described with the compliment that she played like a man.

Tharpe continued her recording career during World War II, and she was one of only two gospel artists to record V-discs for the troops overseas. In 1944 she recorded what has been called the first rock and roll record; the song "Strange Things Happening Every Day" featured Tharpe's vocals and her skills with a resonator guitar. Decca chose Sammy Price, a boogie-woogie pianist, to back her, along with bass and drums. It was the first gospel record to become a hit on the race record charts, a term used for what later became the R&B chart. In 1945 the song reached number two on *Billboard*'s race chart. Other artists who have recorded versions of the song include Johnny Cash, Tom Jones, and Michele Shocked.

By 1946 Tharpe had married her second husband, the promoter Foch Allen. By most accounts, Allen's main interest relative to his wife's career was the way it could profit him. In the spring of 1946, Tharpe attended a concert in Harlem featuring Mahalia Jackson. It turned out it was another performer, Marie Knight, that caught Tharpe's attention. As Tharpe watched Knight perform, she began to think that the two of them could be a successful duo. Two weeks after the concert, Tharpe turned up at Knight's home, contract in hand; Knight accepted the offer, anxious for a concert tour.

According to Tharpe's biographer, although she was excited about performing with Knight, she may have had other reasons for abandoning a solo act. When the two began working together, she was finalizing her divorce from Allen and may have been in search of companionship. It is a fact that before the duo would go their separate ways, they would both be denying rumors in the gospel community that they had entered into a romantic and sexual relationship.

Tharpe was determined to have the new duo record as soon as possible. After rehearsing together, the two were confident enough to schedule a recording audition for Decca. They sang, among other numbers, "Beams of Heaven" for a label executive Paul Cohen. Knight recalled that she heard Cohen say during the session, "that's the girl we want." Very quickly, a contract was prepared and the two signed with Decca.

It didn't take long for the duo to experience success. That summer, their first hit, "Let It Rain," was released to critical and commercial acclaim. The song tells the Great Flood story and features a Tharpe guitar solo. The music critic Nat Hentoff would compare the duo's trading of "swift, crisp choruses" to a bebop performance by Dizzy Gillespie and Roy Eldridge.

Other hits would follow, including "Up Above My Head" and "Gospel Train." "Up Above My Head" was straight rhythm and blues highlighted by Tharpe's work on the guitar. The two women also toured the gospel circuit during these years, which often took them to the southern states. Often in these states, the duo faced both insults and inconveniences. Most restaurants and hotels were closed to them. They were also targets for harassment by both the white population and police. Knight would remember Mississippi as a "gorgeous" state but also call it "one of the most dangerous" places in the country.

In *Shout, Sister, Shout,* Wald describes a typical performance. Tharpe comes out on stage first, dressed in a white satin gown. Picking up her electric guitar, she sang a few of her hits, including "Strange Things Happening Every Day." Knight, also dressed in a gown, joins her, sitting at the piano as they deliver a few of their hit songs. Next, Rosetta moves to the piano, and Knight performs a couple of solos. The duo then slips into the "Saint and Sinner" part of the performance. Tharpe enters in her gown with her guitar. Knight follows, dressed in a straw hat and jeans, carrying a ukulele. The two ham it up until Knight rushes off stage, quickly dons her gown, and returns to perform a big hit, perhaps "Up Above My Head." The audience goes crazy and calls out for more as the duo leaves the stage.

In 1949 their popularity began to wane as Mahalia Jackson surpassed Tharpe in popularity. In addition, Knight desired to perform as a solo act and lost her mother and her children in a house fire. A sure sign that the partnership had ended came when Tharpe performed in Richmond, where she had purchased a home without Knight. Instead, she was backed by the Twilight Singers, who she would rename the Rosettes. They became her background singers when she performed in concert.

By this time, Irwin and Israel (Izzy) Field, sons of Jewish immigrants, were the most successful gospel music promoters in the area extending from Baltimore to Norfolk. It is unclear who sought out who, but what is definite is that the brothers began promoting Tharpe's appearances. Looking to create a concert that would be remembered, the brothers set their sights on having Tharpe perform at Griffith Stadium, the home ballpark of the Washington Senators in 1950. Since Tharpe and Knight had recently reunited to record "When I Take My Vacation in Heaven," the Fields intended to call the show a special reunion concert.

Irwin Field knew that, unlike her mother, Tharpe was not an evangelist, so conducting a revival in the stadium was not an option. Still, he wanted something bigger than an ordinary concert, and he came up with the idea to combine the show with a wedding featuring Tharpe as the star of both events. Field went to Tharpe and said, "Rosetta, find a husband. We'll promote the wedding." Tharpe liked the idea, signed a contract, and promised to find a husband within seven months.

Tharpe had found the man who would be her third husband by the spring. His name was Russell Morrison, and he was described as a handsome man two years younger than his soon-to-be wife. He wasn't gifted musically, but he had always been attracted to entertainers. In 1941 he had landed a position as a valet for the Ink Spots. According to Tharpe's biographer, she likely met him when she was on the road. Although Tharpe was personally pleased and excited about her choice, few who knew her concurred. Marie Knight, for example, thought, and it turns out correctly, that he was just after Tharpe's money. Irwin Field shared this view, and though he would be producing the wedding, he decided the choice of the groom was none of his business.

Although Janis Joplin is usually singled out as the first American woman who could be called a "stadium rocker," one would have to ignore the success of Tharpe's wedding concert at Griffith Stadium to reach such a conclusion. The event drew at least 25,000 paying customers. After an elaborate wedding ceremony that included a twenty-minute wedding party procession, the concert followed. Tharpe performed wearing her wedding dress, singing and playing the electric guitar backed by the Rosettes.

The concert concluded with fireworks that included a reproduction of Tharpe playing her guitar. It is worth noting that although she had made numerous memorable recordings over the years, the wedding concert is one thing that was universally referenced in all her obituaries. In at least one way, this seems appropriate in that Tharpe was exceptional before a live audience. The music promoter Willy Leiser, who befriended her in the sixties, recalled, "above all, she had an exceptional stage presence."

In 1957 the British trombonist Chris Barber booked Tharpe for a month-long tour of the United Kingdom. Tharpe was thrilled about the chance to tour abroad. Other musicians had told her about the appreciative audiences, good treatment for black performers lacking in the United States, and a mainstream press that took a special interest in visiting entertainers. She wasn't disappointed as from the moment she arrived in London, reporters greeted and followed her as if she was visiting royalty. The tour itself was a commercial and critical success.

One of the most memorable performances took place on December 9 in Manchester. Introducing one song, she urged the audience to sit quietly and receive it (the song) because it's wonderful. She then delivered a performance designed to receive the exact opposite of a quiet reception. Using her voice like the instrument it was, she launched into the number changing the words, inserting "ohs and ahs," taking the song and treating it as a puzzle that she dismantled and then reassembled. When she finished, the audience responded with more than a minute of applause. Backed by the Chris Barber Band, Tharpe was undoubtedly the star. The British press noted that she consistently outplayed her hosts.

Encouraged by her British reception, Tharpe began touring the European continent, where her performances were also hailed. In 1958 she toured Scandinavia with an English band Diz Disley. The drummer for the band was a young redhead named Ginger Baker, who a little more than a decade later would make quite a name for himself as a member of the bands Cream and Blind Faith. Baker remembered meeting Tharpe for the first time when they were in rehearsals. Tharpe approached the young man saying, "Hey honey, I love your hair color. What dye do you use?" Baker said that it was his natural color. Tharpe responded, "You'll have to drop your pants to prove it." Baker recalled being Tharpe's favorite during shows and the star giving him huge smiles during performances when she was singing the show-stopping "Didn't It Rain." Looking back on the tour, Baker said, "I loved her."

During these tours, Tharpe began influencing the growing British blues revival. Even performing what were considered gospel songs, her use of the electric guitar, playing it very loudly, and drawing out the notes suggested contemporary rock and roll. Many young British rockers coming of age during the sixties point to Tharpe as a major influence.

Thanks to the European tours, Tharpe's finances were in excellent shape, and she and her husband moved to Philadelphia, where she purchased a home. From 1959 to 1962, she released five albums and fifty-six songs during this period. Two of the albums, *Sister on Tour* and *The Gospel Truth,* were recorded on the jazz label Verve. Ella Mitchell, who, along with the group the All-Stars, provided backing vocals on *The Gospel Truth*, said that Tharpe took control of the recording session, which was completed in a single day.

Back in England in 1964, Tharpe continued attracting young fans. That came as no surprise to her. In 1957 she had been quoted in the *London Daily Mirror* saying, "All this new stuff they call rock and roll, why I've been playing that for years now." During the tour in 1964, the young English boys sporting Beatle haircuts enthusiastically greeted her. In 1992 Graeme Edge, the drummer for the Moody Blues, said, "We had heard the original rock and roll, Buddy Holly, Elvis, Gene Vincent, Little Richard, the Everly Brothers, and Chuck Berry. We put all of that together and, at the same time, discovered another 30 years of American experience on record, Sonny Terry, Brownie McGee, Sister Rosetta Tharpe, and all those people. Then we repackaged it and sold it back in a very free approach."

That spring, Tharpe toured England as part of the American Folk, Blues, and Gospel Caravan with a group of performers, including Muddy Waters. The tour was successful and included a television special. The special concluded with Tharpe leading the other performers in doing their own version of "He's Got the Whole World in His Hands."

Tharpe's grave

Tharpe continued to tour through the sixties. In 1967 at the Newport Folk Festival, she played the piano while her mother, Katie Bell, sang until they practically had to drag her off the stage. Shortly thereafter, Katie Bell, who was in her eighties, passed away after suffering a stroke. Tharpe's mother had been her strongest supporter. She was more than just a mother, as she had been a protector and a collaborator over the years. Those close to Tharpe noticed she took the loss extremely hard. After her mother's death, she cut back on her touring.

By 1970 Tharpe's health was failing. That year her performances were curtailed after she suffered a stroke. Then one of her legs was amputated due to complications stemming from diabetes. On October 9, 1973, the day before a planned recording session, she suffered another stroke and passed away. She was laid to rest in Philadelphia's Northwood Cemetery.

The list of entertainers Tharpe influenced is a long one. When Johnny Cash gave his induction speech at the Rock and Roll Hall of Fame, he referred to Tharpe as his favorite singer. Little Richard shared that opinion. In 1947 Tharpe heard Richard sing before her performance at the Macon City Auditorium. She invited the boy on stage to sing with her. It was his first public performance outside of church. After the show, she paid him, and Little Richard says that inspired him to become a performer.

In 1998 the United States Postal Service honored Tharpe by issuing a commemorative stamp. In 2007 she was inducted into the Blues Hall of Fame. In 2008 a concert was held to raise funds to place a marker on her grave, and January 11 was declared Sister Rosetta Tharpe Day in Pennsylvania. A gravestone was placed on her tomb later that year. In 2018 Tharpe was inducted into the Rock and Roll Hall of Fame as an early influence.

In 2017 National Public Radio aired a show covering Tharpe's career. It concluded with these remarks. She "was a gospel singer at heart who became a celebrity by forging a new path musically . . . Through her unforgettable voice and gospel swing crossover style, Tharpe influenced a generation of musicians, including Aretha Franklin, Chuck Berry, and countless others . . . She was, and is, an unmatched artist."

25

Grover Washington Jr.

"The Smooth Jazzman"

County: Montgomery • Town: Bala Cynwyd
Buried at West Laurel Hill Cemetery
215 Belmont Avenue

He grew up surrounded by music. He would become one of the most popular soul and jazz saxophonist of all time. He would write much of his material and later be recognized as an arranger and a producer. He is widely considered to be one of the founders of the smooth jazz genre. While some jazz critics found his music to be simplistic, he became one of the most commercially successful saxophonists in history. His name was Grover Washington Jr.

Washington was born in Buffalo, New York, on December 12, 1943. His father played the saxophone and was a collector of jazz records. His mother was in the church choir. He grew up listening to his father's records. When he was ten years old, his dad gave him a saxophone. He would practice on his own, and by the time he was twelve, he was playing in clubs.

As he grew older, Washington played with a group from the Midwest who went by the clever name The Four Clefts. His next band was called the Mark III Trio. He was then drafted into the U. S. Army. It was in the army that he met a drummer from New York by the name of Billy Cobham. Cobham was an established New York musician, and he introduced Washington to other musicians from the Big Apple. After he was discharged, Washington exhibited his talents in New York before heading to Philadelphia in 1967, where he became closely identified with that city. Leon Spencer released two albums in the early '70s, and Washington appeared on both.

A Grover Washington, Jr. album cover.

Then Washington caught a break when another sax musician was unable to make a recording date. Washington stepped in and played impressively. This led to Washington's first solo album *Inner City Blues*. The record showcased his talent with the soprano, alto, tenor, and baritone saxophones. He was becoming known as an up and coming jazz artist.

In the early '70s, he released three albums that made him a force in the world of jazz and soul music. In 1974 he released his fourth album *Mister Magic*, and it became a major commercial success. The record made it to number ten on the Billboard charts, and the title track made it to number sixteen on the R&B singles chart. His next album, *Feels So Good*, also made it to number ten on Billboard.

In the late '70s, Washington signed with Elektra Records, which was part of the Warner Music Group. In 1980 he released *Winelight* the record that many believe to represent his best effort. Washington loved basketball, and he was a big fan of the Philadelphia 76ers, which led to him dedicating the second track on the record "Let It Flow" to Julius Erving. He also occasionally played the national anthem before the 76ers games. The high point of the album *Winelight* was his work with the soul artist Bill Withers on the song "Just the Two of Us." That song was a major hit and reached number two on the charts and won a Grammy in 1982 for Best R&B Song; it was also a Song of the Year nominee. The album which went platinum won the Grammy for Best Jazz Fusion Performance. *Winelight* was also nominated for record of the year.

In the 1980s, Washington moved toward the jazz mainstream. Among the artists he worked with was Herbie Hancock. He also released the first album of music from the *Cosby Show*. During a 1989 interview, Washington said, "There's a record player playing in here all the time." At the time, he was pointing at his head. "I'm listening to everything. The screech of brakes. Three or four people walking, and you can hear their heels clicking. Railroad tracks."

Gravesite of the noted smooth jazz man.

Grover Washington Jr.

In 1996, he played at President Clinton's 50th birthday celebration at Radio City Music Hall. Clinton later said, "Grover Washington was as versatile as any jazz musician in America moving with ease and fluency from vintage jazz to funk, and from gospel to blues to pop." Washington once said, "I want to be able to visit any genre and converse there with my horn." Noting that quote Clinton added, "Grover Washington did exactly that, and beautifully."

On December 17, 1999, Washington performed four songs for the *Saturday Early Show* on CBS. While waiting in the green room, he collapsed and was rushed to a local New York hospital where he died that evening. It was determined that he had suffered a massive heart attack. He was laid to rest in West Laurel Hill Cemetery. He was 56 years old.

26

August Wilson

"The Century Cycle"

County: Allegheny • Town: Pittsburgh
Buried at Greenwood Cemetery
321 Kittanning Pike

August Wilson was an American playwright who carved his signature on American theater by capturing the changing texture of black life in America in a series of ten plays, each covering a different decade of the twentieth century. The plays are known as the "Pittsburgh Cycle," also often referred to as his "Century Cycle."

When Wilson began writing his plays, he had little experience with theater, having only seen two plays, and having no formal training. Unencumbered by theatrical history, Wilson created his own rules for his plays. "I wanted to present the unique particulars of black American culture as the transformation of impulse and sensibility into codes of conduct and response, into cultural rituals that defined and celebrated ourselves as men and women of high purpose," Wilson said of his work. He did, and the skill with which he did it won him two Pulitzer Prizes, a Tony Award, and seven New York Drama Critics Circle Awards, in addition to twenty-three honorary degrees.

Wilson's rise from humble beginnings to Broadway was remarkable. He was born Frederick August Kittel on April 27, 1945, In the Hill District community of Pittsburgh. He was the son of Daisy Wilson, an African American cleaning woman, and Frederick Kittel, a German immigrant and baker who was mostly absent from Wilson's life. Daisy raised Wilson and his five siblings in a two-room, cold water apartment above a grocery store at 1227 Bedford Avenue. It's been reported that

August Wilson

August Wilson

Wilson's grandmother walked from Spear, North Carolina, where her family worked as sharecroppers, to Pittsburgh in search of a better life. Daisy managed to keep her children clothed and fed. When Daisy divorced Wilson's father and married David Bedford, the family moved to the white working-class neighborhood of Hazelwood, where they encountered a lot of racial hostility.

In 1959 Wilson entered Central Catholic High School, where he was the victim of constant race-based bullying and abuse. The next year he transferred to Connelly Trade School, where he felt unchallenged and transferred to Gladstone High School in Hazelwood. He quit Gladstone in 1960 after a teacher accused him of plagiarizing a twenty-page paper he wrote on Napoleon. He hid his decision from his mother and continued his education informally at the Carnegie Library of Pittsburgh, where he became a voracious reader. His extensive use of the Carnegie Library resulted in it later awarding him an honorary high school diploma.

By his late teens, Wilson had dedicated himself to the task of becoming a writer. His mother wanted him to become a lawyer and got fed up with him working at odd jobs and kicked him out of the house. He enlisted in the US Army for three years but somehow got himself discharged a year later. He moved into a boarding house at the age of twenty and began writing in bars, cafes, and a local cigar store. He wrote on paper bags, napkins, and yellow note pads and later typed them up at home.

Wilson officially erased his connection to his birth father when he adopted his mother's name in 1965. The symbolic starting point of Wilson's writing career came that same year when he purchased a used typewriter, paying for it with twenty dollars that his sister gave him for writing her a rush term paper on Robert Frost and Carl Sandberg. He decided he was a poet and submitted work to such magazines as *Harpers*. Although some of Wilson's poems were published in some small magazines over the next few years, he failed to achieve recognition as a poet.

In the late 1960s, Wilson joined a group of poets, educators, and artists who formed the Centre Avenue Poets Theater Workshop. Wilson met friend and collaborator Rob Penny through this group, and in 1968, they co-founded the Black Horizon Theater, a community-based theater company in the Hill District of Pittsburgh. It focused on politicizing the community and raising black consciousness. Black Horizons gave Wilson the chance to present his early plays, mostly in public schools and community centers.

In 1969 Wilson married Brenda Burton, a Muslim, and converted to Islam and had a daughter Sakina. He never fully embraced the religion, which contributed to the failure of the marriage, and they divorced in 1972.

In 1978 he went to St. Paul, Minnesota, to visit a friend, Claude Purdy, and decided to stay. Purdy helped him get a job writing educational scripts for the Science Museum of Minnesota and urged Wilson to write a play. In ten days of writing, while sitting in a fish and chips restaurant, Wilson finished a draft of *Jitney*, a play set in a gypsy-cab station. He submitted the play to the Minneapolis Playwrights Center and was awarded a $200 a month fellowship. The next year, in 1981, Wilson married Judy Oliver, a social worker, and quit the job at the museum to devote more time to writing. *Jitney* premiered at the Allegheny Repertory Theater in Pittsburgh and was accepted into the 1982 National Playwrights Conference. It became one of the Pittsburgh Cycle plays reflecting the 1970s.

Wilson's next break came when he met Lloyd Richards, artistic director and dean of the Yale Drama School. Wilson's play *Ma Rainey's Black Bottom* caught Richards' attention at a conference at the Eugene O'Neill Center in Waterford, Connecticut. Richards was the first black director of a Broadway play, *Raisin in the Sun* in 1959. *Ma Rainey* tapped into Wilson's interest in the Blues and its importance in American black history. Set in 1927, the play dealt with how black singers were exploited by whites. *Ma Rainey's Black Bottom* opened on Broadway at the Cort Theatre in 1984 with Lloyd Richards directing. It enjoyed a run of 276 performances and won the New York Drama Critics Circle Award for Best Play of the Year. Thus began a long collaboration between the seasoned director and the novice playwright. Richards went on to direct all of Wilson's plays and served as spokesperson and promoter for Wilson, who once described their relationship as that of a boxer and a trainer.

In 1987 Wilson struck gold with *Fences*. It opened on Broadway in March with James Earl Jones in the starring role. It ran for 525 performances and earned Wilson a Tony Award for Best Play as well as his first Pulitzer Prize for Drama.

Soon after *Fences* opened, Wilson added a second production on Broadway when *Joe Turner's Come and Gone* opened. It won the New York Drama Critic's Circle Award.

In 1990 *The Piano Lesson* opened on Broadway and won Wilson his fourth New York Drama Critic's Circle Award and his second Pulitzer Prize, becoming only the seventh playwright to win more than once. Also, that year Wilson divorced Judy Oliver and moved to Seattle. In 1994 Hallmark Hall of Fame produced a teleplay of *The Piano Lesson*, starring Charles Dutton and Alfred Woodard.

The successful runs on Broadway continued with *Two Trains Running* in 1992, *Seven Guitars* in 1996, *King Hedley II* in 1999, and *Gem of the Ocean* in 2004. *Two Trains Running* and *Seven Guitars* both won New

York Drama Critic's Circle Awards, bringing his total to six, and when *Jitney* opened in New York in 2000, he was awarded his seventh.

In 1994 Wilson tried marriage again to costume designer Constanza Romero. The couple had a daughter Azula Carmen Wilson in 1997.

In 2005 *Radio Golf,* the last play in the Century or Pittsburgh Cycle premiered on April 22 at the Yale Repertory Theatre. Critics praised the play as a triumph, but discussion of the play was overshadowed in the press by public concern for Wilson's health, which had begun to decline. In June, he was diagnosed with liver cancer. On October 2, 2005, August Wilson died in a Seattle hospital. His funeral service was held at Soldiers and Sailors Memorial Hall in Pittsburgh, and he was buried in Greenwood Cemetery.

The American theater community publicly mourned his passing. On October 17, just two weeks after his death, the Virginia Theater on Broadway was renamed the August Wilson Theater in his honor. Also, in February 2006, the African American Cultural Center of Greater Pittsburgh officially became the August Wilson Center for African American Culture. In 2007, the Bedford Avenue home of his youth was declared a historic landmark by the state of Pennsylvania and placed on the National Register of Historic Places in 2013.

The *New York Times* wrote, "Heroic is not a word one uses often without embarrassment to describe a writer or playwright, but the diligence and ferocity of effort behind the creation of his body of work is really an epic story."

Wilson insisted he never wrote exclusively for blacks or whites, or any particular target audience. While one of his primary goals was to place African American culture front and center in a world where blacks had historically been forced to the social sidelines, he was perhaps most interested in taking a look at the human experience. Wilson knew any audience member of any color, could find some way to relate to the struggles and successes of his characters. Actor Denzel Washington, who starred in a 2010 revival of *Fences*, once noted that, though the events in Wilson's plays might appear to be specific to African American life, the overall themes are, in fact, universal.

August Wilson's grave

Washington reprised his role in the 2016 film adaptation of *Fences*. He also produced and directed it. The film was nominated for four Oscars and won two Golden Globes. It was chosen as a top ten film of 2016 by the American Film Institute and grossed $64 million.

"I don't write particularly to effect social change," Wilson once said, "I believe writing can do that, but that's not why I write. I work as an artist. All art is political in the sense that it serves someone's politics."

Bibliography

Books, Magazines, Journals, Files:

Asante, Molefi Kete. *100 Greatest African Americans: A Biographical Encyclopedia.* New York: Prometheus Books, 2002.

Brady, Kathleen. *Lucille: The Life of Lucille Ball.* New York: Hyperion, 1994.

Farrell, Joe and Joe Farley. *Keystone Tombstones Volume One.* Mechanicsburg, PA: Sunbury Press, 2020.

————. *Keystone Tombstones Volume Two.* Mechanicsburg, PA: Sunbury Press, 2020.

————. *Keystone Tombstones Volume Three.* Mechanicsburg, PA: Sunbury Press, 2020.

————. *Keystone Tombstones Volume Four.* Mechanicsburg, PA: Sunbury Press, 2021.

————. *Gotham Graves Volume One.* Mechanicsburg, PA: Sunbury Press, 2020.

————. *Gotham Graves Volume Two.* Mechanicsburg, PA: Sunbury Press, 2020.

Gioia, Ted. *The History of Jazz.* New York: Oxford University Press, 2021.

Grodin, Charles. *It Would Be So Nice If You Weren't Here : My Journey through Show Business.* New York: Vintage Books, 1989.

Haskins, James, and N. R. Mitgang. *Mr. Bojangles: The Biography of Bill Robinson.* New York: Linus Multimedia, 2014.

Holiday, Billie, and Iris Menéndez. *Lady Sings the Blues.* Barcelona: Tusquets, 2015.

Kane, Larry. *Lennon Revealed.* England: Running Press (PA), 2005.

Kennedy, John F. *Profiles in Courage.* New York: Harper, 2003.

Life Magazine (editors). *Lucille Ball: Her Life, Love and Legacy.* New York: Life, 2021.

Martin, Nicholas, and Jasper Rees. *Florence Foster Jenkins: The Inspiring True Story of the World's Worst Singer.* New York: St. Martin's Griffin, 2016.

Sales, Soupy. *Soupy Sez!: My Zany Life and Times.* M. Evans & Company, 2003.

The Rolling Stone Encyclopedia of Rock and Roll. New York: Rolling Stone Press, 1983.

Wald, Gayle. *Shout Sister Shout!: The Untold Story of Rock-And-Roll Trailblazer Sister Rosetta Tharpe.* Boston: Beacon Press, 2007.

Zehme, Bill. *Lost in the Funhouse: The Life and Mind of Andy Kaufman.* New York: Delta, 2009.

Movies and Television Shows:

Angels in America. Directed by Mike Nichols. New York: Home Box Office, 2003.

Beau James. Directed by Melville Shavelson. Hollywood: Paramount Pictures, 1957.

Florence Foster Jenkins. Directed by Stephen Frears. London: BBC Films, 2016.

Lady Sings the Blues. Directed by Sidney J. Furie. Hollywood: Paramount Pictures, 1972.

Man on the Moon. Directed by Miloš Forman. Hollywood: Universal Pictures, 1999.

Rebel Without a Cause. Directed by Nicholas Ray. Los Angeles: Warner Brothers, 1955.

Bibliography

The Men Who Made the Movies: Season 1, Episode 4. Directed by Richard Schickel. Simi Valley, California: Public Broadcasting Service, 1973.

Online Resources:
Ancestry.com – Family tree information and vital records.
Emmys.com – The Emmy Awards site.
Esquire.com – *Esquire Magazine*.
FamousAmericans.net – for information on many individuals.
FindaGrave.com – for burial information, vital statistics and obituaries.
HollywoodReporter.com – The *Hollywood Reporter* newsletter.
IMDB.com – Internet Movie Database.
Legacy.com – Online obituaries.
Mediaconfidential.blogspot.com – Radio industry information.
Newspapers.com – Hundreds of newspaper articles were accessed—too numerous to mention here.
NYTimes.com – The *New York Times* site.
Observer.com – *Observer Magazine*.
Press.uillinois.edu – University of Illinois Press.
ReadingEagle.com – The *Reading Eagle* newspaper.
TeachingAmericanHistory.com – for information on many individuals.
TheHistoryJunkie.com – for information on many individuals.
USHistory.org – for information on many individuals.
Wikipedia.com – for general historical information.

Other Resources:
Fred Rogers Center, Latrobe, Pennsylvania – Information about Fred Rogers.

Index

Index

Index

Index

Index